The Catholic Handbook for
Visiting the Sick and Homebound

2019
Year C

Mary Heinrich

LTP
LITURGY
TRAINING
PUBLICATIONS

Nihil Obstat
Reverend Mr. Daniel G. Welter, JD
Chancellor
Archdiocese of Chicago
April 25, 2018

Imprimatur
Very Reverend Ronald A. Hicks
Vicar General
Archdiocese of Chicago
April 25, 2018

THE CATHOLIC HANDBOOK FOR VISITING THE SICK AND HOMEBOUND 2019 © 2018 Archdiocese of Chicago: Liturgy Training Publications, 3949 South Racine Avenue, Chicago, IL 60609; 800-933-1800; fax 800-933-7094; email: orders@ltp.org; website: www.LTP.org. All rights reserved.

This book was edited by Victoria M. Tufano, Víctor R. Pérez was the production editor, Anna Manhart was the designer, and Kari Nicholls was the production artist. The interior art is by Sister Mary Grace Thul, OP.

Printed in the United States of America

ISBN 978-1-61671-385-0

VS19

CONTENTS

THE GOSPELS AND EXPLANATIONS
OF THE READINGS

Ordinary Time during Summer and Fall

Psalm 23

The LORD is my shepherd;
there is nothing I lack.

In green pastures he makes me lie down;
to still waters he leads me;
he restores my soul.

He guides me along right paths
for the sake of his name.

Even though I walk through the valley
    of the shadow of death,
I will fear no evil, for you are with me;
your rod and your staff comfort me.

You set a table before me
in front of my enemies;
You anoint my head with oil;
my cup overflows.

Indeed, goodness and mercy will pursue me
all the days of my life;
I will dwell in the house of the LORD
for endless days.

INTRODUCTION

Come to me, all you who labor and are burdened, and I will give you rest. Take my yoke upon you and learn from me, for I am meek and humble of heart; and you will find rest for yourselves. For my yoke is easy, and my burden light.

—Matthew 11:28–30

Suffering wears a thousand faces, and every face is Christ's. When we suffer sickness, loss, violence, or the harsher effects of aging in ourselves or in those we love, we cannot really understand the reasons, but we can choose the rock on which we will stand. We are members of the Body of Christ. Christ our Head is present in our suffering. In our dying we share his death. His voyage through death to the glory of the Resurrection becomes our journey. In him, we are held securely in the face of the anxiety, fear, anger, guilt, and grief that sickness, aging, or suffering can bring.

One of the deepest causes of suffering experienced by those whom sickness or aging confines to the narrow world of home, hospital, or geriatric facility is a sense of isolation. We may feel misunderstood, rejected, abandoned by the healthy world of which we were a part, even by those who love us, even by God. We feel that there is something wrong with us. We feel no longer useful. We cause other people discomfort and inconvenience. We may know how we "ought" to pray in times of suffering, but we can't seem to do it. We can't even go to church.

When we have suffered traumatic loss or violence, we may suffer a similar sense of loneliness. Our experience has set us apart. We may feel that no one can understand what we have endured. We find ourselves unable to take an interest in the world of everyday concerns about which others are busy. We may even find ourselves ill at ease with our ordinary companions in faith and worship. Even God may seem to have withdrawn to a safe distance. Our usual forms of prayer no longer seem to suffice. We have questions that are difficult to answer: Why me? Why has God allowed this to happen? We may be angry with God and ashamed of our anger. On the other hand, we may find ourselves more deeply in communion with the suffering Christ or with his bereaved and sorrowful Mother than before, yet separated from others by the intensity of our spiritual experience.

Ministers of care, both lay and the ordained, are sent to step across the chasm that isolates the sufferers, bringing them the comfort of personal presence and prayer. Ministries of care are as diverse as the parishes that sponsor them. Some parishes may have full-time lay pastoral associates or other employees who specialize in pastoral care. These laypeople may have been specially trained. They may have participated in pastoral care internships (Clinical Pastoral Education), or sought degrees in pastoral care or received diocesan or national certification. Parishes may also be fortunate enough to have volunteers who provide pastoral care to those in hospitals, hospices, nursing homes, prisons, police stations, crisis centers, and to those who are dying or have lost a loved one. These volunteers can provide music, proclaim Scripture, offer words of consolation and hope, or simply give the gift of silent presence.

The most familiar ministry of care is that of extraordinary minister of Holy Communion. The word *extraordinary* can be confusing. In this case, the Church uses it officially to distinguish between ordained bishops, priests, and deacons, who are the *ordinary* ministers of Holy Communion, and specially commissioned laypeople who fill the gaps, so to speak, when there are not enough ordinary ministers to give Holy Communion to everyone at Mass or to take Holy Communion to the sick and the homebound. The words *extraordinary* and *ordinary* as they are used here may seem odd because they recall a time when there were so many priests that there was no need for laypeople to take on this role.

This handbook is specially designed for the use of lay ministers of care, so it does not contain the rites for the Sacraments of Penance or the Anointing of the Sick, or the special prayers and blessings used by ordained bishops, priests, or deacons. All lay ministers who provide care to those who are sick, homebound, isolated, or suffering in some way will benefit from the contents of this book.

You, as a minister of care, have been called to be a sign and a bridge. Sent by the parish, you are the living witness that the community of faith and worship has not forgotten the absent sick, the invisible elderly, and the unseen sufferers. Praying with them as a representative of Christ living in the Church, you are a sign that God is and wants to be with them. You draw them back into awareness of their communion with the whole Body of Christ. They, and in many cases their caregivers, discover through you that they are not alone.

The Church has provided two official books containing a wealth of rites for those who visit, pray with, or bring Holy Communion to the sick, aging, dying, or others who are struggling with addiction, personal violence, or the loss of a child through miscarriage—especially those cut off from full participation in the liturgical life of their local Church or parish. These ritual books are called *Pastoral Care of the Sick: Rites of Anointing and Viaticum* and the *Book of Blessings*. *Pastoral Care of the Sick* contains rites specific to those who are sick and dying, providing orders of prayer for visits to the sick and for the Sacraments of Eucharist, Penance, and Anointing of the Sick. The *Book of Blessings* provides multiple orders of blessing for various needs and occasions. What you have in your hand, *The Catholic Handbook for Visiting the Sick and Homebound 2018*, is a booklet containing all of the rituals from *Pastoral Care of the Sick* and the *Book of Blessings* that can be used by laypeople when visiting the sick and the homebound. Everything you will need is right here! You will be able to use this book when you are sent to give Holy Communion to other parishioners or pray with those who are confined to their homes, to hospitals, or to geriatric centers; those who have suffered the traumatic loss of a child through miscarriage; those who suffer from addictions; and those who have been victims of violence. The most important resource you have as a minister, though, is your personal relationship with Christ, our healer and our Savior. You too are the face of Christ.

USING THIS BOOK

The Catholic Handbook for Visiting the Sick and Homebound 2018 will tell you what the Church asks of you, as her spokesperson, to say and do when you visit, pray with, or give Holy Communion to those who suffer. You need not worry about making up prayers—they are provided here for you! In fact, except where the rite itself calls for adaptation, you must use the prayers as they are written because they express the common faith of the Catholic Church to which we all committed ourselves in Baptism.

CONTENTS OF THIS BOOK

You, as a minister of care, will be called upon to offer those whom you visit an opportunity to benefit from the strengthening power of prayer by making use of one of the many rites and orders of prayer and blessing provided by the Church. This book contains everything you will need to give Holy Communion and lead further rites for praying with the sick and others who suffer for various reasons. The rites and prayers are divided into three sections:

- Section 1: Blessings of and Visits to the Sick and Suffering

- Section 2: Holy Communion

- Section 3: Pastoral Care of the Dying

Each of these sections contains the official rites and orders of prayer as provided by the Church in both the *Book of Blessings* and *Pastoral Care of the Sick: Rites of Anointing and Viaticum*.

Blessings of and Visits to the Sick and Suffering

Visiting and Blessing the Sick.   You may be sent to visit the sick simply to pray with them. However, sometimes you may be prepared to give Holy Communion, but you discover that those you are visiting are unable to receive for some reason. At still other times, you may be visiting Catholic patients in an institution, but others who are not Catholic recognize you as a minister and ask you to pray with them. You need not turn away, feeling that you have nothing to offer. These are just a few of the situations when you could use these rites for visiting the sick and the suffering—either to prepare them to receive Holy Communion during a later visit or simply to enable them to draw strength and comfort from the healing presence of Christ.

Titles of These Rites.   Some clarification about the titles of the services contained in this book is needed to prevent confusion. The book titled *Pastoral Care of the Sick: Rites of Anointing and Viaticum* provides two rites for visiting the sick: "Visits to the Sick" and "Visits to a Sick Child." "Visits to the Sick" is used with adults. These two rites from *Pastoral Care of the Sick* are simple prayers for visiting the sick. The *Book of Blessings* also provides two rites. These two rites are "Order for the Blessing of Adults" and "Order for the Blessing of Children." Here the word "order" simply means "order of service." These two "orders" present an entire service of optional song, Scripture, prayer, and blessing.

The Rites.   The "Orders for the Blessing of the Sick" begin with a simple Sign of the Cross and invitation to pray followed by a reading of the Word of God whereas "Visits to the Sick" begins with the reading. "Visits to the Sick" continues with the Lord's Prayer and a choice of concluding prayers designed to address some of the different circumstances in which the sick might find themselves. Consider your options in relation to the situation of the person you are visiting. If you happen to be visiting someone who isn't Catholic, you may use this order of service, but remember to remind them tactfully that Catholics end the Lord's Prayer after "deliver us from evil." If not, be prepared for them to add the longer ending, "for thine is the kingdom, the power and the glory" before the "Amen." Above all, you do not want to cause distress to anyone.

In the "Orders for Blessing of the Sick," the Word of God may be followed with an explanation of the reading, then a litany of intercession. The Church urges the minister to encourage the sick to participate in Christ's redemptive work by uniting their sufferings to his and by praying for the needs of the world. Prayer for others is an effective antidote to the self-preoccupation to which sickness and aging can tempt us. Intercessions provide an excellent way to meet this need. You may allow participants the opportunity to add petitions of their own, but beware of causing embarrassment by prolonging the silence if it becomes clear that they have nothing to say.

Both the rites for "Visits to the Sick" and "Orders for the Blessing of the Sick" end with prayers of blessing which may be said over the person who is ill. The "Orders for the Blessing of the Sick" provides two prayers of blessing. The first option is for more than one person, whereas the second option is for a single individual. The rite stipulates that the minister is to make the Sign of the Cross on the forehead of the sick while saying the prayer. The gesture may be unexpected or unfamiliar, especially coming from a lay minister, so it is wise to let people know what you are preparing to do. The Sign of the Cross may be followed by a prayer for the protection of the Blessed Virgin Mary. The rite suggests singing a familiar Marian song. If music is unavailable, only sing if those you are visiting are able to participate.

"Orders for the Blessing of the Sick" and "Visits to the Sick" end with a concluding prayer. In both rites, the "lay minister invokes the Lord's blessing on the sick and all present by signing himself or herself with the Sign of the Cross."

"Visits to the Sick" includes two prayers of blessing, one for a sick person and one for the elderly. Please note that the lay minister does not make the same gesture as given in "Orders for the Blessing of the Sick." Simply say the prayer.

The "Order for the Blessing of Children" and "Visits to a Sick Child" follow the same pattern as those used for adults, but they use simpler language. You will have to decide which rite or order of blessing is appropriate to use with older children. A word of caution: Before you make the Sign of the Cross on the child's head during the blessing, it would be wise to alert parents or caregivers to see if they have any objections. It is also wise to explain this to the child. Remember that very sick children may have experienced unpleasant medical procedures and may fear the unexplained touch of an unfamiliar adult.

Visiting and Blessing Those Who Suffer. *The Catholic Handbook for Visiting the Sick and Homebound* contains three additional services for blessing those who suffer and may not be able to participate in Sunday Eucharist:

- Blessing a Person Suffering from Addiction or from Substance Abuse

- Blessing a Victim of Crime or Oppression

- Blessing Parents after a Miscarriage

You may meet people in need of one of these special blessings. You may meet them in a health care setting. For example, a patient may have been hospitalized as a result of addictive behavior or alcohol and drug abuse. Sometimes you may meet a patient who has suffered personal violence, such as domestic abuse, rape, a drive-by shooting, injuries sustained in an accident caused by a drunk driver or at the hands of those engaged in criminal activities such as robbery, or a person afflicted with posttraumatic stress disorder. You may also find that a woman has suffered a miscarriage, and she and the father are grieving together. You may also find people among the families of those you are visiting who ask you to pray with them or give them Holy Communion at home or in an institutional environment. An elderly person might indicate a child or grandchild who is suffering one of these needs and ask you to pray with them. You may be among those assigned to special ministries of care in settings such as support groups.

Be aware that the reason for the need may be recent or long standing. Sometimes, someone who is coping with illness, confinement in a geriatric facility, or other situation which has brought you to them will want to discuss something that happened long ago and continues to haunt them. Periods of inactivity brought on by sickness or aging give us plenty of time to think and may spur us to make peace with the past in a new way. These orders of blessing offer that opportunity.

Whenever you meet someone in one of these situations, you may use the appropriate order of blessing from the pages that follow. All of them follow the same pattern: an introductory rite (Sign of the Cross, simple greeting, optional introduction), reading and response, including the opportunity to comment on the reading, intercessions, the Lord's Prayer, a prayer of blessing directed to the particular needs of participants, and a concluding rite (general blessing). The Church encourages adaptation, provided the order of service is followed and the major elements included. For example, you might want to personalize the opening introduction, following the general pattern of the one provided here. Here is one example of a personalized introduction to the "Order for Blessing a Victim of Crime or Oppression." Imagine that you are praying with and for a young woman who is a victim of date rape. You might say something like this:

God has always shown care and compassion for people who have suffered acts of violence, like the one that has brought you here. We commend you, [N.: use the woman's name], to God, who binds up all our wounds, heals us from the pain of betrayal, and restores us to our rightful dignity as a child of God.

The introduction now refers to the victim's own experience, uses her name, and avoids language that could summon up frightening images of being held by a male person.

You will want to choose those intercessions that are most appropriate. You may invite participants to add their own, and you may also do so. Turning one's own suffering into prayer for others is both a way of uniting oneself with the redemptive suffering of Christ and a means of turning one's attention outward. If you are accustomed to using the "Orders for Blessing of the Sick," please note that there are some differences between them and these orders of blessing for those otherwise in distress. In particular, these latter orders call for the Lord's Prayer, which often provides the comfort of a familiar prayer; and they do not call for the minister to touch the person while saying the prayer of blessing for them. This can be an important courtesy when using this order for blessing with those who have suffered personal violence and shy away from being touched by strangers, even in prayers of blessing.

Like the "Orders for the Blessing of the Sick," these orders also provide a shorter form: a short invitation to prayer, a short reading, and a prayer of blessing. These short forms are particularly useful when ministering to those who have very recently experienced a crisis in addiction, an incident of violence, or a miscarriage, and are too distressed to concentrate on a longer ritual. They are also helpful when you are visiting the person for some other reason and find a need to help them deal with one of these issues.

One of the hidden benefits of the Church's rites of prayer is that they teach us to think in harmony with the Church. If you have never experienced the particular need for which you are blessing someone, your good intentions may sometimes stumble in trying to find the right words of comfort. It is easy to offend without meaning to by offering what sound like platitudes to those who are in the immediate throes of suffering. It is also easy to give impressions of God that hurt rather than help them. The texts of these rites will assist you to reflect on how to focus your comments. They are also impersonal enough that they offer room for participants in the rites to take them as words from God to be pondered and applied to their own experience rather than as personal remarks about their own faith response to what they have suffered. Ministers must be particularly careful not to suggest when they speak spontaneously that the sufferer is being punished for a lack of faith or for slack religious practice or for some particular sin. Remember that anger with God, fear of God, a sense of alienation from God, and particularly a sense of despair often lurk at the edges of suffering. You want to encourage instead turning to God in trust and in hope. Even there, though, please be careful to allow room for those who want to turn to God in a positive way but are not yet emotionally ready to do so. God's love is profoundly patient.

Holy Communion

This book provides two rites for lay ministers to give Holy Communion to the sick: "Communion in Ordinary Circumstances" and "Communion in a Hospital or Institution."

Communion in Ordinary Circumstances.   The first form, called "Communion in Ordinary Circumstances," is especially useful if you are taking Holy Communion to the sick or aging in their homes. It assumes two things: First, that you have enough time to lead the full rite of Holy Communion, including a short Liturgy of the Word; second, that those you visit are well enough to participate in a full service. The Church urges us always to consider the needs of the sick or aging. If they are very weak or tire quickly, it's better to shorten or omit elements like the explanation after the reading or the Universal Prayer or Prayer of the Faithful, or simply to use the shorter form called "Communion in a Hospital or Institution" even in a home setting.

Communion in a Hospital or Institution. This second form, "Communion in a Hospital or Institution," provides a minimal format mainly intended for use when you are visiting many patients individually in an institutional setting. The Church expresses a strong preference for avoiding this abbreviated format even in an institution. Instead, it is suggested that, if possible, you gather several residents together in one or more areas and celebrate the full rite of "Communion in Ordinary Circumstances." If that is not possible, the Church recommends that you add elements from the fuller rite, such as the reading of the Word, unless participants are too weak. On the other hand, in the case of extremely sick people, you may shorten "Communion in a Hospital or Institution" by omitting as much of the rite as necessary. Try to include at least a greeting, the Lord's Prayer, the customary responses that precede Holy Communion itself, and the closing prayer. Please note that the "customary responses" have now been reworded. See the section on page 18 on using the new translation from the third edition of *The Roman Missal* for those prayers taken from the Order of Mass for use in the Rites of Communion.

Pastoral Care of the Dying

Viaticum, Holy Communion for the Dying. Any of the seriously ill, but especially hospice patients, may move more quickly than expected toward death. A person who faces death within days should receive Holy Communion under the form of Viaticum. *Viaticum* means something like "travel with you," but it is often translated as "food for the journey." Although the Sacrament of Anointing of the Sick strengthens us in the face of sickness, Eucharist as Viaticum is the sacrament that, together with Penance, prepares a person for the final journey through death to everlasting life in Christ. Catholics are obligated to receive Viaticum if possible. The Sacrament of Anointing of the Sick may be given after Penance but before Viaticum. If the person is unable to swallow, they may receive the

Sacrament of Anointing from a priest instead of Viaticum; however, the Church teaches that Viaticum is the essential sacrament when we are in the face of death. The time for using the special comforting and strengthening prayers of the Rite of Viaticum to administer Holy Communion is while the person is still conscious and able to swallow. Once death has become imminent, dying persons may receive Viaticum every day for as long as they are able. An extraordinary minister of Holy Communion may and should give Viaticum to the dying. If the dying person has not received sacramental absolution, please make sure the person has the opportunity for both the Sacrament of Penance and, if desired, Anointing of the Sick.

Commendation for the Dying and Prayers for the Dead.   While the sacraments, especially Viaticum, unite the dying with Christ in his passage from this life to the next, we also gather with the dying and those around them to sustain this union through the prayer and faith of the Church.

"Commendation for the Dying" does not follow a fixed pattern. You may select any texts from the prayers, litanies, aspirations, psalms, and readings, or you may use other familiar prayers, such as the Rosary. If you have had the opportunity to talk with the dying person and loved ones or others present, choose texts you think will sustain and strengthen them according to their spiritual needs and other circumstances. Pray the texts slowly and quietly, allowing ample opportunities for silence. You may repeat them as often as needed, especially prayers that have special meaning for those present. Even those who are unconscious and dying can sometimes hear more than we realize. If the dying cannot hear, loved ones present will find comfort in the prayers.

If you minister in an institutional setting, you may find that those who are not Catholic will ask you to pray with and for them. You may use these texts with and for any who are in need of the consolation of prayer. The texts drawn from the Bible are especially likely to bring comfort.

Once death has occurred, you will find both prayers for the dead and prayers for family and friends on page 133, "Prayers for the Dead."

Ritual Preparation.   All of the rites are simple to follow. Look them over before making your visits in order to familiarize yourself with the order of prayer. Directions are included and parts are clearly marked so that you can easily lead the assembly in prayer.

The Gospel for Sundays and Holydays of Obligation

Following the rites is the Gospel for Sundays and Holydays of Obligation for Year C. The Church has a three-year cycle of readings. In 2019, the readings will be from Year C. It is recommended to use the Sunday Gospel during the rites for Holy Communion as one important way of uniting the communicants in spirit with the parish from which sickness or age has separated them.

In this book, the Gospel is clearly labeled by date and the title of particular observances so that you can easily find the appropriate reading. For example, if you make your visit during the Second Week of Lent, you will use the Gospel for the Second Sunday of Lent. In 2019, this Sunday of Lent is March 17. Simply look for the date and the title of the celebration and you will know which Gospel to use. For some observances, such as Palm Sunday, the Lectionary provides a longer and shorter form of the Gospel. For simplicity, only the shorter form is included in this resource.

If you are visiting on a Holyday of Obligation, use the Gospel prescribed for these days. You can also locate the Gospel for Holydays of Obligation by date and title. In the dioceses of the United States of America, the Holydays of Obligation occurring in the 2019 liturgical year are:

- Solemnity of the Immaculate Conception of the Blessed Virgin Mary (December 8, 2018)

- Solemnity of the Nativity of the Lord (December 25, 2018)

- Solemnity of Mary, the Holy Mother of God (January 1, 2019)

- Solemnity of the Ascension of the Lord (May 30 or June 2, 2019)

- Solemnity of All Saints (November 1, 2019)

If you are visiting very young sick children, you might want to obtain a copy of the appropriate reading from the *Lectionary for Masses with Children* from your parish. Another option is to read the Gospel passages recommended in "Visits to a Sick Child."

If you are praying with those who are struggling with addictions, the aftermath of violence, or with parents who have suffered the loss of a child through miscarriage, you will usually find the readings recommended in the orders of blessing more appropriate to their circumstances than the Gospel for the Sunday. However, if appropriate, feel free to use the Gospel for Sundays and Holydays of Obligation. To discern which readings to use, it is best to look over the order of service before the visit occurs.

Explanation of the Readings

You will notice that the rites offer an opportunity for the minister of care to give a brief explanation of the reading with special reference to the experience of those with whom you are praying and, where appropriate, of their caregivers. If you are using the Sunday or Holyday reading, you might want to base your explanation of the reading on the parish Sunday Homily in order to deepen the sense of connection you are trying to encourage. If you feel uncomfortable about speaking, you will find a brief explanation of the reading after the Gospel for each Sunday and Holyday. If you choose to read it from the book, it would be a good idea to ponder it and make it your own so that the words come from your heart and not merely from the page. The Word of God itself creates a bond between reader and hearers, breaking down the sense of isolation that afflicts sufferers. Explanatory words that are spoken, or even read, with sincerity and personal conviction will support this pastoral relationship more effectively than words read mechanically.

Patron Saints

Finally, there is a list of saints who the Church has identified as particular intercessors, companions, and guides for those suffering various kinds of afflictions, whether physical or emotional. If you feel that those with whom you pray would welcome the company and support of a saint, you might want to include the saint's name in the intercessions and suggest that those you are visiting continue to ask for the saint's help. An example of an intercession is:

> For all those who suffer from throat cancer, especially **N.** (insert the name of the person or persons present), that through the intercession of Saint Blaise, they may find comfort and strength, we pray to the Lord.

This book does not provide any information about the saints listed, but there are many books and websites where you can find their stories. Such resources are *Companion to the Calendar, Second Edition* (Liturgy Training Publications) and *Butler's Lives of the Saints* (published by The Liturgical Press).

Beyond the Book

The official rites offer appropriate prayers and clear directions, but they don't tell you everything you need to know in order to lead the rituals effectively. Here are some practical hints that may help.

Getting from the Parish Church to Your Pastoral Assignment

Scheduling a Visit.   Some parishes assign ministers to visit particular people but encourage them to make their own arrangements regarding the day and time. Both those in need of your ministry and their families or caregivers, at home or in institutional facilities, appreciate being able to negotiate appropriate times for a pastoral visit or Holy Communion. It gives them an opportunity to make sure that they and those they would like to have present can be there. For example, if you're visiting the sick, you don't want to drop in when patients are absent from their rooms for tests or treatments.

If you are asked to take Holy Communion to the sick and the homebound at times other than during Sunday Mass, please make sure your training includes information about where to find the tabernacle key and how to approach the tabernacle reverently, open it, and transfer the hosts you will need from the ciborium in which they are kept to the container you will use to carry the Blessed Sacrament to the sick (see below). It is particularly important to arrange with the parish coordinator a convenient time for you to obtain the tabernacle key, because it is not permitted to keep the Eucharist at home or carry it all day as you go about your ordinary business before visiting communicants.

Ordinarily, when taking the Blessed Sacrament from the tabernacle, you would pray briefly before the tabernacle, wash your fingers in a small vessel of water that is usually kept beside the tabernacle for that purpose, wipe them on a finger towel also usually kept there, and genuflect after opening the tabernacle. If your parish does not provide either the small vessel or finger towel, wash your hands in the sacristy or otherwise clean your fingers as best you are able over the sacrarium (a sink flowing directly into the ground for water from purifications, from the first washings of the altar cloths, or the water containing the completely dissolved consecrated hosts which cannot be properly consumed).

If you have unused hosts left over at the end of your rounds, you must bring them back to the parish church and replace them in the tabernacle.

After closing the tabernacle, you again wash your fingers. You may also cleanse the empty pyx (a dignified vessel, often round, used to carry the consecrated host) in the sacrarium if it appears to contain crumbs. Fill it with water, drink the water, and dry the pyx carefully on a finger towel, if available.

If you wish to avoid having hosts that must be returned, you can give the last few communicants more than one host so that all the hosts are consumed or consume them yourself as part of the Communion Rite during your last visit, provided all the usual requirements for Holy Communion are met. However, you may not simply consume them yourself after your last visit because Holy Communion is always received in the context of public prayer rather than simply as a matter of convenience by the minister alone. Similarly, you may not take the remaining hosts home to return later to the church because the Eucharist must be kept in a tabernacle or other designated locked place of reservation in a church.

Bringing What You Need.   Make a checklist of what you want to have with you before you leave home. You'll find some suggestions below. Don't forget this book! It does happen. If it does, don't panic, and don't fail to keep your appointment. As a precaution, make every effort to memorize the outline of the rites you expect to use or keep a copy of a simple outline in your pocket, wallet, or purse. In this case, do make up your own prayer, but keep it very short and simple. Borrow a Bible or summarize the Gospel in your own words. God works through all our weaknesses and mistakes.

Carrying the Blessed Sacrament.   The Blessed Sacrament is carried in the pyx or in another dignified vessel reserved exclusively for that purpose. Your parish will probably supply you with what you need. Some pyxes can be worn or carried in a pouch on a cord around the neck. When you are carrying the Blessed Sacrament, remember and attend reverently to Christ, choosing your activities appropriately, without becoming artificially silent or stilted in your conversation, especially with those who are not aware of what you are carrying or of its significance. On the one hand, avoid distractions such as loud music, "talk" programs or other television shows, movies or DVDs/tapes, or other things that would disturb prayer while you are en route. On the other hand, while avoiding such distractions, be careful not to be rude to people who greet you or speak to you in passing as you walk to your destination. Christ is not offended by the company and conversation of human beings! You should make your Communion visit immediately upon leaving the Church.

Music Preparation. Sometimes it might be possible to incorporate music into your visits. Music most certainly can be included in the rites and orders of blessing. Singing familiar melodies and texts can be extremely comforting and healing to those who are suffering. Hospitals, nursing homes, and other facilities might have a piano or you might bring a guitar. A capella singing can be just as effective. Be sure to select music in which either the refrain is simple or the melodies are familiar. Choose texts that give a message of the hope we have in Christ. Here are some suggestions: "Blest Are They" (Haas), "Jesus, Heal Us" (Haas), "Healer of Our Every Ill" (Haugen), "Lord of All Hopefulness" (traditional), "I Heard the Voice of Jesus Say" (traditional), "Remember Your Love" (Balhoff), "Shepherd Me, O God" (Haugen), and "You Are Mine" (Haas).

Preparing an Environment for Prayer: Encountering Christ in Persons

Church ministry is always personal. It is important that you spend a few minutes at the beginning of your visit to get to know those present and give them a chance to feel comfortable with you. Your parish may be able to supply you with helpful information in advance.

When you arrive, put those present at ease by engaging in a few moments of personal conversation. Tell them your name and remind them that the parish has sent you. Ask how they are and listen attentively to their answers. If you are visiting the sick, show your interest and concern, but remember that you are not there to offer medical advice or to pass judgment on medical matters, even if you yourself are a professional medical caregiver. If you can, address those you are visiting by name, but be aware that not everyone likes to be addressed by a first name without permission. Sickness, debilitating aging, and other forms of public suffering often rob people of their sense of personal dignity, so treating people with respect is an important dimension of your ministry. Whatever their condition, you and they are both collaborators in Christ's work. Ministry is a two-way street: those whom you visit are serving you by their witness to Christ's suffering as much as you are serving them by offering them Christ's loving comfort. Take note of any special needs you see: is the sufferer low on energy, in pain, limited in motion, hard of hearing, angry, sad, or seemingly depressed? You will want to tailor the length, content, and style of the celebration accordingly.

Preparing Yourself to Lead Prayer

The world of the suffering, especially those confined to home or, even more so, to a hospital or geriatric facility may not feel much like a place of prayer. The most important element in creating an environment for prayer is you. The minister who prays while leading others in prayer is the most powerful invitation one can offer to those who need to be called from all the preoccupations of suffering into deeper awareness of the mystery of God present and acting in our midst.

Here are some steps you can take to develop this important skill:

- Devote time to praying, reading, and meditating on the texts of the prayers and readings provided in this book. You will best pray them in public if you have already prayed them many times in private.

- Familiarize yourself thoroughly with the structure and flow of the rites so that you can concentrate on the people rather than the book. You need not memorize prayers or readings. Simply know what comes next and where to find it.

- Before you go into the building or room, pray briefly, asking Christ to work through you; after the visit, pause to give thanks.

- Reflect on your experience after you return home. Were there moments during the celebration when you felt uncertain or distracted? Why? What could you do next time to make yourself more at ease so that you can pray more attentively without losing contact with those you are leading in prayer? Sharing experience with other ministers of care or parish staff can be a useful way to continue and deepen everyone's ministry formation.

Preparing the Room for Prayer

You can also take some simple steps to establish an atmosphere that encourages prayer when circumstances allow. A small standing crucifix, cross, or icon heightens consciousness of Christ. Appropriate lighting can help, where possible. In an institutional setting, for example, a lamp or sunlight creates a more calming environment than do fluorescent lights. If you are taking Holy Communion to someone, take a small white cloth and a candle with you to prepare a place to put the pyx containing the Blessed Sacrament as a focus for the celebration as you lead the other prayers. (Be sure you have something with which to light the candle!) A corporal (traditionally a square, white, linen cloth upon which is placed sacred vessels holding the Blessed Sacrament) is not required, but if it is used, it is traditionally placed on top of another white cloth rather than on a bare surface. Caregivers familiar with the rite may have prepared a place in advance, but many will not.

Be aware of the restrictions you may face in a health care or geriatric facility. The rites for Holy Communion recommend that the minister be accompanied by a candle-bearer and place a candle on the table where the Blessed Sacrament will stand during the celebration, as described above. However, safety regulations usually forbid the use of open flames in institutions. Oxygen and other substances that might be in use are highly flammable. Moreover, you may not be able to find any appropriate surface other than a bedside table or night stand that will have to be cleared before you can set up a place for the Blessed Sacrament. Be prepared to make whatever practical adjustments the circumstances require. If you have never visited a particular hospital unit or nursing home, see if you can find another minister who has and find out what to expect.

Preparing Participants for Prayer

After a few moments of conversation, find a graceful way to end the social part of the visit without seeming uninterested or abrupt. Then give the participants a simple, brief overview of the rite you will be using so they will know what to expect, unless you know they are already familiar with the rite. Surprises tend to disrupt prayer! It's especially important to decide in advance who will do the reading. The directions say that the reading may be done "by one of those present or by the minister." If you don't know the participants, the best solution might be to ask for a volunteer (and allow the volunteer a few moments to prepare), but remember that not everyone is willing or able to read in public with short notice, especially in times of distress. Finally, mark the beginning of prayer clearly by inviting silent attentiveness, making the Sign of the Cross and moving into the service itself.

Recognizing the Recipient

You are ministering not only to those to whom the ritual is addressed but also to those around them, whether loved ones or caregivers. Be sure to include them by looking at them and speaking to them, as well as to the person who is your focus. When you are saying prayers of blessing over the sufferer, your attention is on that person alone, but all present are invited to join in the "Amen" that affirms and concludes the prayer. Practice with another minister until you can say prayers in such a way that others know when and how to respond without having a book in front of them.

Who May Receive Holy Communion?

Catholic shut-ins, caregivers, or others who assemble with them may receive Holy Communion provided the usual conditions have been met. You can offer that invitation before you begin the rite for Holy Communion, being careful not to embarrass or offend those who are not eligible to receive. "The elderly, the infirm and those who care for them can receive the Holy Eucharist even if they have eaten something within the preceding hour" (*Code of Canon Law*, 919 §2).

Special Circumstances

Unfortunately, neither sickness nor the deterioration sometimes brought on by aging is neat or predictable. The physical, psychological, and spiritual condition of those you visit may have changed since the arrangements for your visit were made. You may need to make unprepared changes in the rite or blessing you are using to meet the current need.

Special Circumstances for Extraordinary Ministers of Holy Communion

If you are taking Holy Communion to the sick or elderly, sometimes those you are visiting will express reluctance to receive. They may or may not want to tell you why. They might be embarrassed to say that they are too nauseated; they might feel alienated from God; they might need sacramental absolution but don't want to say so. You are obviously a person of generosity and compassion, or you wouldn't have volunteered to be an extraordinary minister of Holy Communion. However, a Holy Communion visit is not ordinarily the best time to identify and try to resolve serious personal or spiritual problems. Be aware of your status and of the vulnerability of the suffering: You represent the Church, and you have more power than you may realize to make others feel guilty by showing that you disapprove of their decision not to receive Holy Communion or by giving the impression that they have wasted your time. Remember that they are not rejecting you as a person. Rather, they are struggling with something deeper. Offer to pray with them, using the rites provided for visiting or blessing the sick. Invite them to enter more deeply into communion with the suffering and risen Christ who loves them. Let them know what pastoral resources are available to them: offer to return or to send another minister at a more convenient time; provide the parish phone number; offer to let the pastoral staff know that they would like a priest to visit, without forcing them to reply. If the parish distributes a bulletin during the weekend Masses, bring one along to leave with the person you are visiting.

Sometimes you may find that those you are visiting are unable to swallow easily. Consult medical caregivers. If they give permission, you may break the host into the smallest of pieces, place a piece on the person's tongue to dissolve, and follow with a glass of water to make swallowing possible. Be careful with crumbs when you break the host. The best thing to do is to break the host carefully over the pyx so that crumbs will fall into the pyx. If any crumbs fall on the cloth or table on which the pyx has been placed, moisten your finger, pick up all the crumbs very carefully, and consume them reverently.

You may even find that someone cannot ingest the host at all. In such cases, the person may receive the Blood of Christ, but that requires specialized vessels and procedures. Report the circumstances to your pastor, parish coordinator, or to the facility chaplain's office if the person is in a health care or geriatric facility. They will be able to give Holy Communion appropriately. In the meantime, use one of the rites for visiting or blessing the sick to give them the support of your presence and prayer.

Be aware that the hospitalized may not be permitted to take anything by mouth for a period of time prior to certain tests or treatments. Even a small piece of the host received at such times may cause medical personnel to cancel the planned procedure. If you see a sign that says "Nothing by mouth" or "NPO," initials for the Latin phrase *nil per os*, meaning the same thing, ask a member of the medical staff if you may administer Holy Communion, but expect a "no." In this case, too, you should still pray with the sick or aging, using one of the rites for visiting or blessing the sick. Remember that you still offer them the comfort of Christ's presence in his Word and through your own presence and that of the parish you represent.

Don't be alarmed by moments of silence. Sometimes ministers think they need to fill silences with conversation or action. There is nothing wrong with sitting in silence with another. In fact, these can be quite healing moments. God is present in the silence.

You should also be cognizant of those who are either not able to speak, have difficulty speaking, or speak rather slowly. Be patient and allow them to respond as they are able.

It is important that the extraordinary minister of Holy Communion keeps in mind the sacramental rites which are an essential part of the Church's ministry to the sick and dying and which can be administered only by an ordained bishop or priest—the Sacraments of Reconciliation and the Anointing of the Sick. As appropriate, it is part of your ministry to bring these to the attention of the sick and those confined to their homes, and if needed, to help them contact a priest.

Using the New Translation

The recent changes in *The Roman Missal* still present some challenges when visiting the ill and homebound. Some of the texts in the rites for the sick and dying were borrowed from the Mass, so they must also be used in the new translation. In collaboration with the United States Conference of Catholic Bishops (USCCB) and the International Commission on English in the Liturgy Corporation (ICEL) this edition of *The Catholic Handbook for Visiting the Sick and Homebound* has been updated with the proper texts.

This change in translation poses two pastoral challenges for ministers of care. The first is to familiarize yourself with the new texts so that you can use them comfortably without awkward pauses or repetitions. Your own sense of ease allows participants to relax and concentrate on receiving Christ prayerfully rather than paying attention to you. It has been suggested that the previous translation of the Mass might be used with those confused by illness, trauma, or age, but that does not seem necessary in celebrations of Communion for such recipients. The changes in the ministers' texts are minimal. The previous texts are probably not particularly familiar to most people because they have never actually had to say them personally. They are unlikely to notice that the texts have a slightly different wording now, as long as you give them the proper cue word for their responses. For example, after you have said, "Behold the Lamb of God, / behold him who takes away the sins of the world. / Blessed are those called to the supper of the Lamb," you can ease participants into the correct response by looking at them, nodding your head, and starting them out on "Lord, I am not worthy . . . " That technique can be useful even with familiar texts that people are not accustomed to reciting solo!

The second challenge requires pastoral sensitivity and discernment. It will take some time for the new translation to become a habit for worshippers. You will sometimes be taking Communion to people who have not been able to attend Mass since the new translations were introduced and so are unfamiliar with them. You will be visiting others who are traumatized by strange surroundings, illness, age, and distress. Under those circumstances, the old texts will come much more easily to mind for many. Please remember that your primary task is pastoral care, not catechesis. If participants make the old responses and you try to correct them, you will introduce a note of uncertainty and discomfort that may keep them from the communion with Christ in prayer that they so badly need. In some cases, you might provide them with participation aids that contain the appropriate responses. However, they may or may not find such aids useful. Not everyone reads easily. Some will have lost track of their glasses. Others may be unable to hold the aids steady enough to read them. The light may be too poor or the text too small for some. You will need to assess the circumstances and make an on-the-spot decision about whether or not to give them whatever aids you may have brought. Fostering prayer is your primary goal. While you yourself must use the correct texts, the correctness of participants' responses is secondary.

Service to the People of God

Among these nuts and bolts of the ministry of care, never lose sight of your purpose. You have been commissioned in the name of Christ and his Church to serve as a bridge builder across the isolation that separates the sick and suffering from the parish community of faith and worship. Your deepest task is to carry the Good News of the Gospel to those who stand in need of its healing power. With your parish or diocesan training program, the support of your parish pastoral staff and other ministers of care, this book, and your growing experience, you have many of the tools you will need. However, the most important tool is one that only Christ can provide for you. The more deeply you yourself enter into the heart of the Gospel message, the more clearly you will see that sick and healthy, young and old, grieving and rejoicing, struggling and at peace, are all one Body.

In that Body, we are all servants of the Good News we proclaim, building one another up in faith and love until that day when, by God's gracious gift, we will all dwell together in the Lord's own house for ever and ever.

Genevieve Glen, OSB
Abbey of St. Walburga
Virginia Dale, Colorado
Revised December 2011

ABOUT THE AUTHOR

Sister Genevieve Glen, OSB, is a Benedictine nun of the contemplative Abbey of St. Walburga in Virginia Dale, Colorado. She holds master's degrees in systematic theology from St. John's University, Collegeville, Minnesota, and in spirituality from the Catholic University of America in Washington, DC, where she also did extensive doctoral studies in liturgy. She has lectured and written extensively on the Church's rites for the sick and dying. She is coauthor of the *Handbook for Ministers of Care, Second Edition* (Liturgy Training Publications) and contributing editor of *Recovering the Riches of Anointing: A Study of the Sacrament of the Sick* (Liturgical Press).

THE RITES

Orders for the Blessing of the Sick

INTRODUCTION

376   The blessing of the sick by the ministers of the Church is a very ancient custom, having its origins in the practice of Christ himself and his apostles. When ministers visit those who are sick, they are to respect the provisions of *Pastoral Care of the Sick: Rites of Anointing and Viaticum,* nos. 42–56, but the primary concern of every minister should be to show the sick how much Christ and his Church are concerned for them.

377   The text of *Pastoral Care of the Sick* indicates many occasions for blessing the sick and provides the blessing for formularies.[13]

378   The present order may be used by a priest or deacon. It may also be used by a layperson, who follows the rites and prayers designated for a lay minister. While maintaining the structure and chief elements of the rite, the minister should adapt the celebration to the circumstances of the place and the people involved.

379   When just one sick person is to be blessed, a priest or deacon may use the short formulary given in no. 406.

---

13.   See Roman Ritual, Pastoral Care of the Sick: Rites of Anointing and Viaticum, no. 54.

ORDER OF BLESSING

A. ORDER FOR THE BLESSING OF ADULTS
INTRODUCTORY RITES

380   *When the community has gathered, the minister says:*

In the name of the Father, and of the Son, and of the Holy Spirit.

All make the sign of the cross and reply:

Amen.

382   *A lay minister greets those present in the following words.*

Brothers and sisters, let us bless the Lord, who went about doing good and healing the sick. Blessed be God now and for ever.

R. *Blessed be God now and for ever.*

Or:

R. *Amen.*

383   *In the following or similar words, the minister prepares the sick and all present for the blessing.*

The Lord Jesus, who went about doing good works and healing sickness and infirmity of every kind, commanded his disciples to care for the sick, to pray for them, and to lay hands on them. In this celebration we shall entrust our sick brothers and sisters to the care of the Lord, asking that he will enable them to bear their pain and suffering in the knowledge that, if they accept their share in the pain of his own passion, they will also share in its power to give comfort and strength.

READING OF THE WORD OF GOD

384   A reader, another person present, or the minister reads a text of sacred Scripture, taken preferably from the texts given in Pastoral Care of the Sick *and the* Lectionary for Mass.[14] *The readings chosen should be those that best apply to the physical and spiritual condition of those who are sick.*

Brothers and sisters, listen to the words of the second letter of Paul to the Corinthians: 1:3–7

The God of all consolation.

Blessed be the God and Father of our Lord Jesus Christ, the Father of compassion and God of all encouragement, who encourages us in our every affliction, so that we may be able to encourage those who are in any affliction with the encouragement with which we ourselves are encouraged by God. For as Christ's sufferings overflow to us, so through Christ does our encouragement also overflow. If we are afflicted, it is for your encouragement and salvation; if we are encouraged, it is for your encouragement, which enables you to endure the same sufferings that we suffer. Our hope for you is firm, for we know that as you share in the sufferings, you also share in the encouragement.

385   Or:

Brothers and sisters, listen to the words of the holy gospel according to Matthew: 11:28–30

Come to me and I will refresh you.

Jesus said to the crowds: "Come to me, all you who labor and are burdened, and I will give you rest. Take my yoke upon you and learn from me, for I am meek and humble of heart;

---

14.   See ibid, no. 297; Lectionary for Mass (2nd ed., 1981), nos. 790–795, 796–800 (Ritual Masses: V. Pastoral Care of the Sick and the Dying, 1. Anointing of the Sick and 2. Viaticum), and nos. 933–937 (Masses for Various Needs and Occasions, III. For Various Public Needs, 24. For the Sick).

and you will find rest for yourselves. For my yoke is easy, and my burden light."

386   *Or:*

**Brothers and sisters, listen to the words of
the holy gospel according to Mark:**   6:53–56
They laid the sick in the marketplace.

After making the crossing to the other side of the sea, Jesus and his disciples came to land at Gennesaret and tied up there. As they were leaving the boat, people immediately recognized him. They scurried about the surrounding country and began to bring in the sick on mats to wherever they heard he was. Whatever villages or towns or countryside he entered, they laid the sick in the marketplaces and begged him that they might touch only the tassel on his cloak; and as many as touched it were healed.

387   *As circumstances suggest, one of the following responsorial psalms may be sung or said, or some other suitable song.*

R. *Lord, you have preserved my life from destruction.*

Isaiah 38
Once I said,
"In the noontime of life I must depart!
To the gates of the nether world I shall be consigned
for the rest of my years." **R.**

I said, "I shall see the LORD no more
in the land of the living.
No longer shall I behold my fellow men
among those who dwell in the world." **R.**

My dwelling, like a shepherd's tent,
is struck down and borne away from me;
You have folded up my life, like a weaver
who severs the last thread. **R.**

Those live whom the LORD protects;
yours . . . the life of my spirit.
You have given me health and life. **R.**

Psalm 102:2–3, 24–25

R. *(v. 2) O Lord, hear my prayer, and let my cry come to you.*

388   *As circumstances suggest, the minister may give those present a brief explanation of the biblical text, so that they may understand through faith the meaning of the celebration.*

INTERCESSIONS

389   *The intercessions are then said. The minister introduces them and an assisting minister or one of those present announces the intentions. From the following intentions those best suited to the occasion may be used or adapted, or other intentions that apply to those who are sick and to the particular circumstances may be composed.*

The minister says:

The Lord Jesus loves our brothers and sisters who are ill. With trust let us pray to him that he will comfort them with his grace, saying:

R. *Lord, give those who are sick the comfort of your presence.*

Assisting minister:

Lord Jesus, you came as healer of body and of spirit, in order to cure all our ills. **R.**

Assisting minister:

You were a man of suffering, but it was our infirmities that you bore, our sufferings that you endured. **R.**

Assisting minister:

You chose to be like us in all things, in order to assure us of your compassion. **R.**

Assisting minister:

You experienced the weakness of the flesh in order to deliver us from evil. **R.**

Assisting minister:

At the foot of the cross your Mother stood as companion in your sufferings, and in your tender care you gave her to us as our Mother. **R.**

Assisting minister:

It is your wish that in our own flesh we should fill up what is wanting in your sufferings for the sake of your Body, the Church. **R.**

390   *Instead of the intercessions or in addition to them, one of the following litanies taken from Pastoral Care of the Sick, nos. 245 and 138 may be used.*

Minister:

You bore our weakness and carried our sorrows:
Lord, have mercy.

R. *Lord, have mercy.*

Minister:

You felt compassion for the crowd, and went about doing good and healing the sick: Christ, have mercy.

R. *Christ, have mercy.*

Minister:

You commanded your apostles to lay their hands on the sick in your name: Lord, have mercy.

R. *Lord, have mercy.*

391   Or:

The minister says:

Let us pray to God for our brothers and sisters and for all those who devote themselves to caring for them.

Assisting minister:

Bless **N.** and **N.** and fill them with new hope and strength: Lord, have mercy.

R. *Lord, have mercy.*

Assisting minister:

Relieve their pain: Lord, have mercy. **R.**

Assisting minister:

Free them from sin and do not let them give way to temptation: Lord, have mercy. **R.**

Assisting minister:

Sustain all the sick with your power: Lord, have mercy. **R.**

Assisting minister:

Assist all who care for the sick: Lord, have mercy. **R.**

Assisting minister:

Give life and health to our brothers and sisters on whom we lay our hands in your name: Lord, have mercy. **R.**

PRAYER OF BLESSING

394   A lay minister traces the sign of the cross on the forehead of each sick person and says the following prayer of blessing.

Lord, our God,
who watch over your creatures with unfailing care,
keep us in the safe embrace of your love.
With your strong right hand raise up your servants
     (*N.* and *N.*)
and give them the strength of your own power.
Minister to them and heal their illnesses,
so that they may have from you the help they long for.

We ask this through Christ our Lord.

R. Amen.

395   Or, for one sick person:

Lord and Father, almighty and eternal God,
by your blessing you give us strength and support
     in our frailty:
turn with kindness toward this your servant *N.*
Free him/her from all illness and restore him/her to health,
so that in the sure knowledge of your goodness
he/she will gratefully bless your holy name.

We ask this through Christ our Lord.

R. Amen.

396   After the prayer of blessing the minister invites all present to pray for the protection of the Blessed Virgin. They may do so by singing or reciting a Marian antiphon, for example, We turn to you for protection (Sub tuum praesidium) *or* Hail, Holy Queen.

Concluding Rite

398   A lay minister invokes the Lord's blessing on the sick and all present by signing himself or herself with the sign of the cross and saying:

May the Lord Jesus Christ,
who went about doing good and healing the sick,
grant that we may have good health
and be enriched by his blessings.

R. Amen.

B. ORDER FOR THE BLESSING OF CHILDREN

399   For the blessing of sick children, the texts already given are to be adapted to the children's level, but special intercessions are provided here and a special prayer of blessing.

Intercessions

400   To the following intentions others may be added that apply to the condition of the sick children and to the particular circumstances.

The minister says:

The Lord Jesus loved and cherished the little ones with a special love. Let us, then, pray to him for these sick children, saying:

R. Lord, keep them in all their ways.

Or:

R. Lord, hear our prayer.

Assisting minister:

Lord Jesus, you called the little children to come to you and said that the kingdom of heaven belongs to such as these; listen with mercy to our prayers for these children. (For this we pray:) *R.*

Assisting minister:

You revealed the mysteries of the kingdom of heaven, not to
the wise of this world, but to little children; give these children
the proof of your love. (For this we pray:) **R.**

Assisting minister:

You praised the children who cried out their Hosannas on
the eve of your Passion; strengthen these children and their
parents with your holy comfort. (For this we pray:) **R.**

Assisting minister:

You charged your disciples to take care of the sick; stand
at the side of all those who so gladly devote themselves to
restoring the health of these children. (For this we pray:) **R.**

PRAYER OF BLESSING

402   *A lay minister, and particularly a mother or father when blessing
a sick child, traces the sign of the cross on each child's forehead and then
says the following prayer of blessing.*

Father of mercy and God of all consolation,
you show tender care for all your creatures
and give health of soul and body.
Raise up these children
    (*or* this child *or* the son/daughter you have given us)
    from their (his/her) sickness.
Then, growing in wisdom and grace in your sight and ours,
they (he/she) will serve you all the days of their (his/her) life
in uprightness and holiness
and offer the thanksgiving due to your mercy.

We ask this through Christ our Lord.
R. *Amen.*

C. SHORTER RITE

403 *The minister says:*

Our help is in the name of the Lord.

All reply:

Who made heaven and earth.

404 *One of those present or the minister reads a text of sacred Scripture, for example:*

2 Corinthians 1:3–4

Blessed be the God and Father of our Lord Jesus Christ, the Father of compassion and God of all encouragement, who encourages us in our every affliction, so that we may be able to encourage those who are in any affliction with the encouragement with which we ourselves are encouraged by God.

Matthew 11:28–29

Jesus said, "Come to me, all you who labor and are burdened, and I will give you rest. Take my yoke upon you and learn from me, for I am meek and humble of heart; and you will find rest for yourselves."

405 *As circumstances suggest . . . a lay minister may trace the sign of the cross on the sick person's forehead while saying the prayer.*

Lord and Father, almighty and eternal God,
by your blessing you give us strength and support
  in our frailty:
turn with kindness toward your servant, **N.**
Free him/her from all illness and restore him/her to health,
so that in the sure knowledge of your goodness
he/she will gratefully bless your holy name.

We ask this through Christ our Lord.

R. *Amen.*

Order for the Blessing of a Person Suffering from Addiction or from Substance Abuse

INTRODUCTION

407   Addiction to alcohol, drugs, and other controlled substances causes great disruption in the life of an individual and his or her family. This blessing is intended to strengthen the addicted person in the struggle to overcome addiction and also to assist his or her family and friends.

408   This blessing may also be used for individuals who, although not addicted, abuse alcohol or drugs and wish the assistance of God's blessing in their struggle.

409   Ministers should be aware of the spiritual needs of a person suffering from addiction or substance abuse, and to this end the pastoral guidance on the care of the sick and rites of *Pastoral Care of the Sick* will be helpful.

410   If the recovery process is slow or is marked by relapses, the blessing may be repeated when pastorally appropriate.

411   These orders may be used by a priest or a deacon, and also by a layperson, who follows the rites and prayers designated for a lay minister.

A. ORDER OF BLESSING
INTRODUCTORY RITES

412   When the community has gathered, a suitable song may be sung. After the singing, the minister says:

In the name of the Father, and of the Son, and of the Holy Spirit.

All make the sign of the cross and reply:

Amen.

414   A lay minister greets those present in the following words:

Let us praise God our creator, who gives us courage and strength, now and for ever.

R. Amen.

415   In the following or similar words, the minister prepares those present for the blessing.

God created the world and all things in it and entrusted them into our hands that we might use them for our good and for the building up of the Church and human society. Today we pray for **N.**, that God may strengthen him/her in his/her weakness and restore him/her to the freedom of God's children. We pray also for ourselves that we may encourage and support him/her in the days ahead.

READING OF THE WORD OF GOD

416   A reader, another person present, or the minister reads a text of sacred Scripture.

Brothers and sisters, listen to the words of the second letter of Paul to the Corinthians: 4:6–9

We are afflicted, but not crushed.

For God who said, "Let light shine out of darkness," has shone in our hearts to bring to light the knowledge of the glory of God on the face of Jesus Christ.

But we hold this treasure in earthen vessels, that the surpassing power may be of God and not from us. We are afflicted in every way, but not constrained; perplexed, but not driven to despair; persecuted, but not abandoned; struck down, but not destroyed.

417   Or:

Isaiah 63:7–9   He has favored us according to his mercy.

Romans 8:18–25—I consider the sufferings of the present to be as nothing compared with the glory to be revealed in us.

Matthew 15:21–28—Woman, you have great faith.

418   As circumstances suggest, one of the following responsorial psalms may be sung or said, or some other suitable song.

***R.** Our help is from the Lord who made heaven and earth.*

Psalm 121

I lift up my eyes toward the mountains;
whence shall help come to me?
My help is from the Lord
who made heaven and earth. ***R.***

May he not suffer your foot to slip;
may he slumber not who guards you:
Indeed he neither slumbers nor sleeps,
the guardian of Israel. **R.**

The LORD is your guardian; the LORD is your shade;
he is beside you at your right hand.
The sun shall not harm you by day,
nor the moon by night. **R.**

The LORD will guard you from all evil;
he will guard your life.
The LORD will guard your coming and your going,
both now and forever. **R.**

Psalm 130:1–2, 3–4, 5–6, 7–8

R. *(v. 5) My soul trusts in the Lord.*

419   As circumstances suggest, the minister may give those present a brief explanation of the biblical text, so that they may understand through faith the meaning of the celebration.

INTERCESSIONS

420   The intercessions are then said. The minister introduces them and an assisting minister or one of those present announces the intentions. From the following those best suited to the occasion may be used or adapted, or other intentions that apply to the particular circumstances may be composed.

The minister says:
Our God gives us life and constantly calls us to new life; let us pray to God with confidence.

R. *Lord, hear our prayer.*

Assisting minister:

For those addicted to alcohol/drugs, that God may be their strength and support, we pray. **R.**

Assisting minister:

For **N.**, bound by the chains of addiction/substance abuse, that we encourage and assist him/her in his/her struggle, we pray. **R.**

Assisting minister:

For **N.**, that he/she may trust in the mercy of God through whom all things are possible, we pray. **R.**

Assisting minister:

For the family and friends of **N.,** that with faith and patience they show him/her their love, we pray. **R.**

Assisting minister:

For the Church, that it may always be attentive to those in need, we pray. **R.**

421   *After the intercessions the minister, in the following or similar words, invites all present to sing or say the Lord's Prayer.*

Let us pray to our merciful God as Jesus taught us:

All:

Our Father . . .

PRAYER OF BLESSING

422   A lay minister says the prayer with hands joined.

A   *For addiction*

God of mercy,
we bless you in the name of your Son, Jesus Christ,
who ministered to all who came to him.
Give your strength to **N.**, your servant,
bound by the chains of addiction.
Enfold him/her in your love
and restore him/her to the freedom of God's children.

Lord,
look with compassion on all those
who have lost their health and freedom.
Restore to them the assurance of your unfailing mercy,
and strengthen them in the work of recovery.

To those who care for them,
grant patient understanding and a love that perseveres.

We ask this through Christ our Lord.
R. *Amen.*

B   *For substance abuse*

God of mercy,
we bless you in the name of your Son, Jesus Christ,
who ministered to all who came to him.
Give your strength to **N.**, your servant,
enfold him/her in your love
and restore him/her to the freedom of God's children.

Lord,
look with compassion on all those
who have lost their health and freedom.
Restore to them the assurance of your unfailing mercy,
strengthen them in the work of recovery,
and help them to resist all temptation.

To those who care for them,
grant patient understanding and a love that perseveres.

We ask this through Christ our Lord.

R. *Amen.*

*As circumstances suggest, the minister in silence may sprinkle the person
with holy water.*

CONCLUDING RITE

424   *A lay minister concludes the rite by signing himself or herself with
the sign of the cross and saying:*

May our all-merciful God, Father, Son, and Holy Spirit, bless
us and embrace us in love for ever.

R. *Amen.*

425   *It is preferable to end the celebration with a suitable song.*

B. SHORTER RITE

426   *All make the sign of the cross as the minister says:*

Our help is in the name of the Lord.

All reply:

Who made heaven and earth.

427   *One of those present or the minister reads a text of sacred Scripture, for example:*

Brothers and sisters, listen to the words of the second letter of Paul to the Corinthians: 4:6–9

We are afflicted, but not crushed.

For God who said, "Let light shine out of darkness," has shone in our hearts to bring to light the knowledge of the glory of God on the face of Jesus Christ.

But we hold this treasure in earthen vessels, that the surpassing power may be of God and not from us. We are afflicted in every way, but not constrained; perplexed, but not driven to despair; persecuted, but not abandoned; struck down, but not destroyed.

428   *Or:*

Isaiah 63:7–9—He has favored us according to his mercy.

Matthew 15:21–28—Woman, you have great faith.

429   *A lay minister says the prayer with hands joined.*

A   *For addiction*

God of mercy,
we bless you in the name of your Son, Jesus Christ,
who ministered to all who came to him.
Give your strength to **N.**, your servant,
bound by the chains of addiction.
Enfold him/her in your love
and restore him/her to the freedom of God's children.

Lord,
look with compassion on all those
who have lost their health and freedom.
Restore to them the assurance of your unfailing mercy,
and strengthen them in the work of recovery.

To those who care for them,
grant patient understanding and a love that perseveres.

We ask this through Christ our Lord.
R. *Amen.*

B　　*For substance abuse*

God of mercy,
we bless you in the name of your Son, Jesus Christ,
who ministered to all who came to him.
Give your strength to **N.**, your servant,
enfold him/her in your love
and restore him/her to the freedom of God's children.

Lord,
look with compassion on all those
who have lost their health and freedom.
Restore to them the assurance of your unfailing mercy,
strengthen them in the work of recovery,
and help them to resist all temptation.

To those who care for them,
grant patient understanding and a love that perseveres.

We ask this through Christ our Lord.
R. *Amen.*

Order for the Blessing of a Victim of Crime or Oppression

INTRODUCTION

430   The personal experience of a crime, political oppression, or social oppression can be traumatic and not easily forgotten. A victim often needs the assistance of others, and no less that of God, in dealing with this experience.

431   This blessing is intended to assist the victim and help him or her come to a state of tranquility and peace.

432   These orders may be used by a priest or a deacon, and also by a layperson, who follows the rites and prayers designated for a lay minister.

A. ORDER OF BLESSING

INTRODUCTORY RITES

433   When the community has gathered, a suitable song may be sung. After the singing, the minister says:

In the name of the Father, and of the Son, and of the Holy Spirit.
All make the sign of the cross and reply:

Amen.

435   A lay minister greets those present in the following words:

May the Lord grant us peace, now and for ever.

R. *Amen.*

436   In the following or similar words, the minister prepares those present for the blessing.

Throughout history God has manifested his love and care for those who have suffered from violence, hatred, and oppression. We commend **N.** to the healing mercy of God who binds up all our wounds and enfolds us in his gentle care.

READING OF THE WORD OF GOD

437   A reader, another person present, or the minister reads a text of sacred Scripture.

Brothers and sisters, listen to the words of the holy gospel according to Matthew: 10:28–33
Do not fear.

Jesus said to his disciples: "Do not be afraid of those who kill the body but cannot kill the soul; rather, be afraid of the one who can destroy both soul and body in Gehenna. Are not two sparrows sold for a small coin? Yet not one of them falls to the ground without your Father's knowledge. Even all the hairs of your head are counted. So do not be afraid; you are worth more than many sparrows. Everyone who acknowledges me before others I will acknowledge before my heavenly Father. But whoever denies me before others, I will deny before my heavenly Father."

438   *Or:*

Isaiah 59:6b–8, 15–18—The Lord is appalled by evil and injustice.

Job 3:1–26—Lamentation of Job.

Lamentations 3:1–24—I am one who knows affliction.

Lamentations 3:49–59—When I called, you came to my aid.

Micah 4:1–4—Every person shall sit undisturbed.

Matthew 5:1–10—The beatitudes.

Matthew 5:43–48—Love your enemies, pray for those who persecute you.

Luke 10:25–37—The good Samaritan.

439   *As circumstances suggest, one of the following responsorial psalms may be sung, or some other suitable song.*

R. *The Lord is my strength and my salvation.*

Psalm 140
Deliver me, O Lord, from evil men;
preserve me from violent men,
From those who devise evil in their hearts,
and stir up wars every day. **R.**

Save me, O Lord, from the hands of the wicked;
preserve me from violent men
Who plan to trip up my feet—
the proud who have hidden a trap for me;
They have spread cords for a net;
by the wayside they have laid snares for me. **R.**

Grant not, O Lord, the desires of the wicked;
further not their plans.
Those who surround me lift up their heads;
may the mischief which they threaten overwhelm them. **R.**

I know that the Lord renders
justice to the afflicted, judgment to the poor.
Surely the just shall give thanks to your name;
the upright shall dwell in your presence. **R.**

Psalm 142:2–3, 4b–5, 6–7
R. (v. 6) You, O Lord, are my refuge.

Psalm 31:2–3a, 4–5, 15–16, 24–25
R. (v. 6) Into your hands I commend my spirit.

440   As circumstances suggest, the minister may give those present a brief explanation of the biblical text, so that they may understand through faith the meaning of the celebration.

INTERCESSIONS

441   The intercessions are then said. The minister introduces them and an assisting minister or one of those present announces the intentions. From the following those best suited to the occasion may be used or adapted, or other intentions that apply to the particular circumstances may be composed.

The minister says:
Let us pray to the Lord God, the defender of the
weak and powerless, who delivered our ancestors from harm.
R. Deliver us from evil, O Lord.

Assisting minister:

For **N.,** that he/she may be freed from pain and fear, we pray to the Lord. **R.**

Assisting minister:

For all who are victims of crime/oppression, we pray to the Lord. **R.**

Assisting minister:

For an end to all acts of violence and hatred, we pray to the Lord. **R.**

Assisting minister:

For those who harm others, that they may change their lives and turn to God, we pray to the Lord. **R.**

442   *After the intercessions the minister, in the following or similar words, invites all present to sing or say the Lord's Prayer.*

The Lord heals our wounds and strengthens us in our weakness; let us pray as Christ has taught us:

All:

Our Father . . .

PRAYER OF BLESSING

443   A lay minister says the prayer with hands joined.

Lord God,
your own Son was delivered into the hands of the wicked,
yet he prayed for his persecutors
and overcame hatred with the blood of the cross.
Relieve the suffering of **N.**;
grant him/her peace of mind
and a renewed faith in your protection and care.

Protect us all from the violence of others,
keep us safe from the weapons of hate,
and restore to us tranquility and peace.

We ask this through Christ our Lord.
R. Amen.

As circumstances suggest, the minister in silence may sprinkle the person with holy water.

CONCLUDING RITE

445   A lay minister concludes the rite by signing himself or herself with the Sign of the Cross and saying:

May God bless us with his mercy,
strengthen us with his love,
and enable us to walk in charity and peace.
R. *Amen.*

446   It is preferable to end the celebration with a suitable song.

B. SHORTER RITE

447 *All make the sign of the cross as the minister says:*

Our help is in the name of the Lord.

All reply:

Who made heaven and earth.

448 *One of those present or the minister reads a text of sacred Scripture, for example:*

Brothers and sisters, listen to the words of the holy gospel according to Matthew: 10:28–33

Do not fear.

Jesus said to his disciples: "Do not be afraid of those who kill the body but cannot kill the soul; rather, be afraid of the one who can destroy both soul and body in Gehenna. Are not two sparrows sold for a small coin? Yet not one of them falls to the ground without your Father's knowledge. Even all the hairs of your head are counted. So do not be afraid; you are worth more than many sparrows. Everyone who acknowledges me before others I will acknowledge before my heavenly Father. But whoever denies me before others, I will deny before my heavenly Father."

449 *Or:*

Isaiah 59:6b–8, 15–18—The Lord is appalled by evil and injustice.

Job 3:1–26—Lamentation of Job.

Lamentations 3:1–24—I am a man who knows affliction.

Lamentations 3:49–59—When I called, you came to my aid.

Matthew 5:1–10—The beatitudes.

Luke 10:25–37—The good Samaritan.

Lord God,
your own Son was delivered into the hands of the wicked
yet he prayed for his persecutors
and overcame hatred with the blood of the cross.
Relieve the suffering of **N.**;
grant him/her peace of mind
and a renewed faith in your protection and care.

Protect us all from the violence of others,
keep us safe from the weapons of hate,
and restore to us tranquility and peace.

We ask this through Christ our Lord.
R. *Amen.*

Order for the Blessing of Parents after a Miscarriage

INTRODUCTION

279   In times of death and grief the Christian turns to the Lord for consolation and strength. This is especially true when a child dies before birth. This blessing is provided to assist the parents in their grief and console them with the blessing of God.

280   The minister should be attentive to the needs of the parents and other family members and to this end the introduction to the *Order of Christian Funerals,* Part II: Funeral Rites for Children will be helpful.

281   These orders may be used by a priest or deacon, and also by a layperson who follows the rites and prayers designated for a lay minister.

A. ORDER OF BLESSING
INTRODUCTORY RITES

*282   When the community has gathered, a suitable song may be sung.
The minister says:*

In the name of the Father, and of the Son, and of the
Holy Spirit.

All make the sign of the cross and reply:

Amen.

284   A lay minister greets those present in the following words:

Let us praise the Father of mercies, the God of all consolation.
Blessed be God for ever.

R. *Blessed be God for ever.*

*285   In the following or similar words, the minister prepares those
present for the blessing.*

For those who trust in God,
in the pain of sorrow there is consolation,
in the face of despair there is hope,
in the midst of death there is life.
N. and **N.**, as we mourn the death of your child
we place ourselves in the hands of God
and ask for strength, for healing, and for love.

READING OF THE WORD OF GOD

286   A reader, another person present, or the minister reads a text of sacred Scripture.

Brothers and sisters, listen to the words of the book of Lamentations: 3:17–26

Hope in the Lord.

My soul is deprived of peace,
I have forgotten what happiness is;
I tell myself my future is lost,
all that I hoped for from the LORD.
The thought of my homeless poverty
is wormwood and gall;
Remembering it over and over
leaves my soul downcast within me.
But I will call this to mind,
as my reason to have hope:
The favors of the LORD are not exhausted,
his mercies are not spent;
They are renewed each morning,
so great is his faithfulness.
My portion is the LORD, says my soul;
therefore will I hope in him.
Good is the LORD to one who waits for him,
to the soul that seeks him;
It is good to hope in silence
for the saving help of the LORD.

287   Or:

Isaiah 49:8–13—In a time of favor I answer you, on the day of salvation I help you.

Romans 8:18–27—In hope we were saved.

Romans 8:26–31—If God is for us, who can be against us?

Colossians 1:9–12—We have been praying for you unceasingly.

Hebrews 5:7–10—Christ intercedes for us.

Luke 22:39–46—Agony in the garden.

288   As circumstances suggest, one of the following responsorial psalms may be sung, or some other suitable song.

R. *To you, O Lord, I lift up my soul.*

Psalm 25

Your ways, O Lord, make known to me;
teach me your paths,
Guide me in your truth and teach me,
for you are God my savior,
and for you I wait all the day. **R.**

Remember that your compassion, O Lord,
and your kindness are from of old.
The sins of my youth and my frailties remember not;
in your kindness remember me
because of your goodness, O Lord. **R.**

Look toward me, and have pity on me,
for I am alone and afflicted.
Relieve the troubles of my heart,
and bring me out of my distress. **R.**

Preserve my life, and rescue me;
let me not be put to shame, for I take refuge in you.
Let integrity and uprightness preserve me,
because I wait for you, O LORD. **R.**

Psalm 143:1, 5–6, 8, 10

R. *(v. 1) O Lord, hear my prayer.*

289   As circumstances suggest, the minister may give those present a brief explanation of the biblical text, so that they may understand through faith the meaning of the celebration.

INTERCESSIONS

290   The intercessions are then said. The minister introduces them and an assisting minister or one of those present announces the intentions. From the following those best suited to the occasion may be used or adapted, or other intentions that apply to the particular circumstances may be composed.

The minister says:

Let us pray to God who throughout the ages has heard the cries of parents.

R. *Lord, hear our prayer.*

Assisting minister:

For **N.** and **N.**, who know the pain of grief, that they may be comforted, we pray. **R.**

Assisting minister:

For this family, that it may find new hope in the midst of suffering, we pray. **R.**

Assisting minister:

For these parents, that they may learn from the example
of Mary, who grieved by the cross of her Son, we pray. **R.**

Assisting minister:

For all who have suffered the loss of a child, that Christ may
be their support, we pray. **R.**

291   *After the intercessions the minister, in the following or similar
words, invites all present to sing or say the Lord's Prayer.*

Let us pray to the God of consolation and hope, as Christ has
taught us:

All:

Our Father . . .

PRAYER OF BLESSING

292   *A lay minister says the prayer with hands joined.*

Compassionate God,
soothe the hearts of **N.** and **N.**,
and grant that through the prayers of Mary,
who grieved by the cross of her Son,
you may enlighten their faith,
give hope to their hearts,
and peace to their lives.

Lord,
grant mercy to all the members of this family
and comfort them with the hope
that one day we will all live with you,
with your Son Jesus Christ, and the Holy Spirit,
for ever and ever.
R. *Amen.*

293   Or:

Lord,
God of all creation
we bless and thank you for your tender care.

Receive this life you created in love
and comfort your faithful people in their time of loss
with the assurance of your unfailing mercy.

We ask this through Christ our Lord.

R. *Amen.*

*As circumstances suggest, the minister in silence may sprinkle the parents
with holy water.*

CONCLUDING RITE

*295   A lay minister concludes the rite by signing himself or herself with
the sign of the cross and saying:*

May God give us peace in our sorrow,
consolation in our grief,
and strength to accept his will in all things.

R. *Amen.*

296   It is preferable to end the celebration with a suitable song.

B. SHORTER RITE

297 *All make the sign of the cross as the minister says:*

Our help is in the name of the Lord.

All reply:

Who made heaven and earth.

298 *One of those present or the minister reads a text of sacred Scripture, for example:*

Brothers and sisters, listen to the words of the book of Lamentations: 3:17–26

Hope in the Lord.

My soul is deprived of peace,
I have forgotten what happiness is;
I tell myself my future is lost,
all that I hoped for from the LORD.
The thought of my homeless poverty
is wormwood and gall;
Remembering it over and over
leaves my soul downcast within me.
But I will call this to mind,
as my reason to have hope:
The favors of the LORD are not exhausted,
his mercies are not spent;
They are renewed each morning,
so great is his faithfulness.
My portion is the LORD, says my soul;
therefore will I hope in him.
Good is the LORD to one who waits for him,
to the soul that seeks him;
It is good to hope in silence
for the saving help of the LORD.

299   Or:

Romans 8:26–31—If God is for us, who can be against us?
Colossians 1:9–12—We have been praying for you unceasingly.

300   A lay minister says the prayer with hands joined.

Compassionate God,
soothe the hearts of **N.** and **N.**,
and grant that through the prayers of Mary,
who grieved by the cross of her Son,
you may enlighten their faith,
give hope to their hearts,
and peace to their lives.

Lord,
grant mercy to all the members of this family
and comfort them with the hope
that one day we will all live with you,
with your Son Jesus Christ, and the Holy Spirit,
for ever and ever.
R. *Amen.*

301   Or:
Lord,
God of all creation,
we bless and thank you for your tender care.
Receive this life you created in love
and comfort your faithful people in their time of loss
with the assurance of your unfailing mercy.

We ask this through Christ our Lord.
R. *Amen.*

Pastoral Care of the Sick

INTRODUCTION

Lord, your friend is sick.

42   The rites in Part I of *Pastoral Care of the Sick: Rites of Anointing and Viaticum* are used by the Church to comfort the sick in time of anxiety, to encourage them to fight against illness, and perhaps to restore them to health. These rites are distinct from those in the second part of this book, which are provided to comfort and strengthen a Christian in the passage from this life.

43   The concern that Christ showed for the bodily and spiritual welfare of those who are ill is continued by the Church in its ministry to the sick. This ministry is the common responsibility of all Christians, who should visit the sick, remember them in prayer, and celebrate the sacraments with them. The family and friends of the sick, doctors and others who care for them, and Priests with pastoral responsibilities have a particular share in this ministry of comfort. Through words of encouragement and faith they can help the sick to unite themselves with the sufferings of Christ for the good of God's people.

    Remembrance of the sick is especially appropriate at common worship on the Lord's Day, during the Universal Prayer at Mass and in the intercessions at Morning Prayer and Evening Prayer. Family members and those who are dedicated to the care of the sick should be remembered on these occasions as well.

44   Priests have the special task of preparing the sick to celebrate the Sacrament of Penance (individually or in a communal celebration), to receive the Eucharist frequently if their condition permits, and to celebrate the Sacrament of Anointing at the appropriate time. During this preparation it will be especially helpful if the sick person, the Priest, and the family become accustomed to praying together. The Priest should provide leadership to those who assist him in the care of the sick, especially Deacons and other ministers of the Eucharist.

The words "Priest," "Deacon," and "minister" are used advisedly. Only in those rites which must be celebrated by a Priest is the word "Priest" used in the rubrics (that is, the Sacrament of Penance, the Sacrament of the Anointing of the Sick, the celebration of Viaticum within Mass). Whenever it is clear that, in the absence of a Priest, a Deacon may preside at a particular rite, the words "Priest or Deacon" are used in the rubrics. Whenever another minister is permitted to celebrate a rite in the absence of a Priest or Deacon, the word "minister" is used in the rubrics, even though in many cases the rite will be celebrated by a Priest or Deacon.

45   The pastoral care of the sick should be suited to the nature and length of the illness. An illness of short duration in which the full recovery of health is a possibility requires a more intensive ministry, whereas illness of a longer duration which may be a prelude to death requires a more extensive ministry. An awareness of the attitudes and emotional states which these different situations engender in the sick is indispensable to the development of an appropriate ministry.

VISITS TO THE SICK

46   Those who visit the sick should help them to pray, sharing with them the word of God proclaimed in the assembly from which their sickness has separated them. As the occasion permits, prayer drawn from the psalms or from other prayers or litanies may be added to the word of God. Care should be taken to prepare for a future visit during which the sick will receive the Eucharist.

VISITS TO A SICK CHILD

47   What has already been said about visiting the sick and praying with them (see no. 46) applies also in visits to a sick child. Every effort should be made to know the child and to accommodate the care in keeping with the age and comprehension of the child. In these circumstances the minister should also be particularly concerned to help the child's family.

48   If it is appropriate, the Priest may discuss with the parents the possibility of preparing and celebrating with the child the Sacraments of Initiation (Baptism, Confirmation, Eucharist). The Priest may baptize and confirm the child (see *Rite of Confirmation,* no. 7b). To complete the process of Initiation, the child should also receive first Communion. (If the child is a proper subject for Confirmation, then he or she may receive first Communion in accordance with the practice of the Church.) There is no reason to delay this, especially if the illness is likely to be a long one.

49   Throughout the illness the minister should ensure that the child receives Communion frequently, making whatever adaptations seem necessary in the rite for Communion of the sick (Chapter III).

50   The child is to be anointed if he or she has sufficient use of reason to be strengthened by the Sacrament of Anointing. The rites provided (Chapter IV) are to be used and adapted.

COMMUNION OF THE SICK

51   Because the sick are prevented from celebrating the Eucharist with the rest of the community, the most important visits are those during which they receive Holy Communion. In receiving the Body and Blood of Christ, the sick are united sacramentally to the Lord and are reunited with the Eucharistic community from which illness has separated them.

ANOINTING OF THE SICK

52   The Priest should be especially concerned for those whose health has been seriously impaired by illness or old age. He will offer them a new sign of hope: the laying on of hands and the Anointing of the Sick accompanied by the prayer of faith (James 5:14). Those who receive this sacrament in the faith of the Church will find it a true sign of comfort and support in time of trial. It will work to overcome the sickness, if this is God's will.

53   Some types of mental sickness are now classified as serious. Those who are judged to have a serious mental illness and who would be strengthened by the sacrament may be anointed (see no. 5). The anointing may be repeated in accordance with the conditions for other kinds of serious illness (see no. 9).

Visits to the Sick

INTRODUCTION

I was sick, and you visited me.

54   The prayers contained in this chapter follow the common pattern of reading, response, prayer, and blessing. This pattern is provided as an example of what can be done and may be adapted as necessary. The minister may wish to invite those present to prepare for the reading from Scripture, perhaps by a brief introduction or through a moment of silence. The laying on of hands may be added by the Priest, if appropriate, after the blessing is given.

55   The sick should be encouraged to pray when they are alone or with their families, friends, or those who care for them. Their prayer should be drawn primarily from Scripture. The sick person and others may help to plan the celebration, for example, by choosing the prayers and readings. Those making these choices should keep in mind the condition of the sick person.

     The passages found in this chapter and those included in Part III speak of the mystery of human suffering in the words, works, and life of Christ. Occasionally, for example, on the Lord's Day, the sick may feel more involved in the worship of the community from which they are separated if the readings used are those assigned for that day in the Lectionary. Prayers may also be drawn from the psalms or from other prayers or litanies. The sick should be helped in making this form of prayer, and the minister should always be ready to pray with them.

56   The minister should encourage the sick person to offer his or her sufferings in union with Christ and to join in prayer for the Church and the world. Some examples of particular intentions which may be suggested to the sick person are: for peace in the world; for a deepening of the life of the Spirit in the local Church; for the pope and the bishops; for people suffering in a particular disaster.

READING

57 The word of God is proclaimed by one of those present or by the minister. An appropriate reading from Part III or one of the following readings may be used:

A *Acts of the Apostles 3:1–10*

In the name of Jesus and the power of his Church, there is salvation—even liberation from sickness.

B *Matthew 8:14–17*

Jesus fulfills the prophetic figure of the servant of God taking upon himself and relieving the sufferings of God's people.

RESPONSE

58 A brief period of silence may be observed after the reading of the word of God. An appropriate psalm from Part III or one of the following psalms may be used:

A *Psalm 102*

R. *O Lord, hear my prayer and let my cry come to you.*

O Lord, hear my prayer,
   and let my cry come to you.
Hide not your face from me
   in the day of my distress.
Incline your ear to me;
   in the day when I call, answer me speedily. **R.**

He has broken down my strength in the way;
    he has cut short my days. I say: O my God,
Take me not hence in the midst of my days;
    through all generations your years endure. **R.**

Of old you established the earth,
    and the heavens are the work of your hands.
They shall perish, but you remain
    though all of them grow old like a garment.
Like clothing you change them, and they are changed,
    but you are the same, and your years have no end. **R.**

Let this be written for the generation to come,
    and let his future creatures praise the Lord:
"The Lord looked down from his holy height,
    from heaven he beheld the earth,
To hear the groaning of the prisoners,
    to release those doomed to die." **R.**

B   *Psalm 27*

R. *The Lord is my light and my salvation.*

The Lord is my light and my salvation;
    whom should I fear?
The Lord is my life's refuge;
    of whom should I be afraid? **R.**

One thing I ask of the Lord;
    this I seek:
To dwell in the house of the Lord
    all the days of my life
That I may gaze on the loveliness of the Lord
    and contemplate his temple. **R.**

For he will hide me in his abode
in the day of trouble,
He will conceal me in the shelter of his tent,
he will set me high upon a rock. *R.*

The minister may then give a brief explanation of the reading, applying it to the needs of the sick person and those who are looking after him or her.

THE LORD'S PRAYER

59   *The minister introduces the Lord's Prayer in these or similar words:*

Now let us offer together the prayer our Lord Jesus Christ taught us:

All say:
Our Father . . .

CONCLUDING PRAYER

60   *The minister says a concluding prayer. One of the following may be used:*

A

O God, who willed that our infirmities
be borne by your Only Begotten Son
to show the value of human suffering,
listen in kindness to our prayers
for our brothers and sisters who are sick;
grant that all who are oppressed by pain, distress
or other afflictions

may know that they are chosen
among those proclaimed blessed
and are united to Christ
in his suffering for the salvation of the world.
Through Christ our Lord.
R. *Amen.*

B

Almighty ever-living God, eternal health of believers,
hear our prayers for your servants who are sick:
grant them, we implore you, your merciful help,
so that, with their health restored,
they may give you thanks in the midst of your Church.
Through Christ our Lord.
R. *Amen.*

C

All-powerful and ever-living God,
we find security in your forgiveness.
Give us serenity and peace of mind;
may we rejoice in your gifts of kindness
and use them always for your glory and our good.

We ask this in the name of Jesus the Lord.
R. *Amen.*

BLESSING

61   The minister may give a blessing. One of the following may be used:

A

All praise and glory is yours, Lord our God,
for you have called us to serve you in love.
Bless **N.**
so that he/she may bear this illness
in union with your Son's obedient suffering.
Restore him/her to health,
and lead him/her to glory.

Through Christ our Lord.
R. *Amen.*

B

For an elderly person

All praise and glory are yours, Lord our God,
for you have called us to serve you in love.
Bless all who have grown old in your service
and give **N.** strength and courage
to continue to follow Jesus your Son.

Through Christ our Lord.
R. *Amen.*

A minister who is not a Priest or Deacon invokes God's blessing and makes the Sign of the Cross on himself or herself, while saying:

May the Lord bless us,
protect us from all evil,
and bring us to everlasting life.

R. *Amen.*

The minister may then trace the Sign of the Cross on the sick person's forehead.

Visits to a Sick Child

INTRODUCTION

Let the children come to me; do not keep them back from me.

62   The following readings, prayers, and blessings will help the minister to pray with sick children and their families. They are provided as an example of what can be done and may be adapted as necessary. The minister may wish to invite those present to prepare for the reading from Scripture, perhaps by a brief introduction or through a moment of silence.

63   If the child does not already know the minister, the latter should seek to establish a friendly and easy relationship with the child. Therefore, the greeting which begins the visit should be an informal one.

64   The minister should help sick children to understand that the sick are very special in the eyes of God because they are suffering as Christ suffered and because they can offer their sufferings for the salvation of the world.

65   In praying with the sick child the minister chooses, together with the child and the family if possible, suitable elements of common prayer in the form of a brief Liturgy of the Word. This may consist of a reading from Scripture, simple one-line prayers taken from Scripture which can be repeated by the child, other familiar prayers such as the Lord's Prayer, the Hail Mary, litanies, or a simple form of the Universal Prayer. The laying on of hands may be added by the Priest, if appropriate, after the child has been blessed.

READING

66   *One of the following readings may be used for a brief Liturgy of the Word. Other readings may be chosen, for example: Mark 5:21–23, 35–43, Jesus raises the daughter of Jairus and gives her back to her parents; Mark 9:14–27, Jesus cures a boy and gives him back to his father; Luke 7:11–15, Jesus raises a young man, the only son of his mother, and gives him back to her; John 4:46–53, Jesus gives his second sign by healing an official's son. In addition, other stories concerning the Lord's healing ministry may be found suitable, especially if told with the simplicity and clarity of one of the children's versions of Scripture.*

A   *Mark 9:33–37*

Jesus proposes the child as the ideal of those who would enter the kingdom.

B   *Mark 10:13–16*

Jesus welcomes the children and lays hands on them.

RESPONSE

67   *After the reading of the word of God, time may be set apart for silent reflection if the child is capable of this form of prayer. The minister should also explain the meaning of the reading to those present, adapting it to their circumstances.*

The minister may then help the child and the family to respond to the word of God. The following short responsory may be used:

Jesus, come to me.

—*Jesus, come to me.*

Jesus, put your hand on me.

—*Jesus, put your hand on me.*

Jesus, bless me.

—*Jesus, bless me.*

THE LORD'S PRAYER

68 *The minister introduces the Lord's Prayer in these or similar words:*

**Let us pray to the Father using those words which
Jesus himself used:**

All say:

Our Father . . .

CONCLUDING PRAYER

69   *The minister says a concluding prayer. One of the following
may be used.*

A

God of love,
ever caring,
ever strong,
stand by us in our time of need.

Watch over your child **N.** who is sick,
look after him/her in every danger,
and grant him/her your healing and peace.

We ask this in the name of Jesus the Lord.
R. *Amen.*

B

Father,
in your love
you gave us Jesus
to help us rise triumphant over grief and pain.

Look on your child **N.** who is sick
and see in his/her sufferings those of your Son.

Grant **N.** a share in the strength you granted your Son
that he/she too may be a sign
of your goodness, kindness, and loving care.

We ask this in the name of Jesus the Lord.
R. Amen.

BLESSING

70   *The minister makes a Sign of the Cross on the child's forehead, saying one of the following:*

A

N., when you were baptized,
you were marked with the Cross of Jesus.
I (we) make this cross ✚ on your forehead
and ask the Lord to bless you,
and restore you to health.

R. Amen.

B

All praise and glory is yours, heavenly God,
for you have called us to serve you in love.
Have mercy on us and listen to our prayer
as we ask you to help **N.**

Bless ✚ your beloved child,
and restore him/her to health
in the name of Jesus the Lord.

R. *Amen.*

Each one present may in turn trace the Sign of the Cross on the child's forehead, in silence.

A minister who is not a Priest or Deacon invokes God's blessing and makes the Sign of the Cross on himself or herself, while saying:

May the Lord bless us,
protect us from all evil,
and bring us to everlasting life.

R. *Amen.*

Communion of the Sick

INTRODUCTION

Whoever eats this bread will live for ever.

71   This chapter contains two rites: one for use when Communion can be celebrated in the context of a Liturgy of the Word; the other, a brief Communion rite for use in more restrictive circumstances, such as in hospitals.

72   Priests with pastoral responsibilities should see to it that the sick or aged, even though not seriously ill or in danger of death, are given every opportunity to receive the Eucharist frequently, even daily, especially during Easter Time. They may receive Communion at any hour. Those who care for the sick may receive Communion with them, in accord with the usual norms. To provide frequent Communion for the sick, it may be necessary to ensure that the community has a sufficient number of Extraordinary Ministers of Holy Communion. The minister should wear attire appropriate to this ministry.

The sick person and others may help to plan the celebration, for example, by choosing the prayers and readings. Those making these choices should keep in mind the condition of the sick person. The readings should help those present to reach a deeper understanding of the mystery of human suffering in relation to the Paschal Mystery of Christ.

73   The faithful who are ill are deprived of their rightful and accustomed place in the Eucharistic community. In bringing Communion to them the Extraordinary Minister of Holy Communion represents Christ and manifests faith and charity on behalf of the whole community toward those who cannot be present at the Eucharist. For the sick the reception of Communion is not only a privilege but also a sign of support and concern shown by the Christian community for its members who are ill.

The links between the community's Eucharistic celebration, especially on the Lord's Day, and the Communion of the sick are intimate and manifold. Besides remembering the sick in the Universal Prayer at Mass, those present should be reminded occasionally of the significance of Communion in the lives of those who are ill: union with Christ in his struggle with evil, his prayer for the world, and his love for the Father, and union with the community from which they are separated.

The obligation to visit and comfort those who cannot take part in the Eucharistic assembly may be clearly demonstrated by taking Communion to them from the community's Eucharistic celebration. This symbol of unity between the community and its sick members has the deepest significance on the Lord's Day, the special day of the Eucharistic assembly.

74   When the Eucharist is brought to the sick, it should be carried in a pyx or small closed container. Those who are with the sick should be asked to prepare a table covered with a linen cloth upon which the Blessed Sacrament will be placed. Lighted candles are prepared and, where it is customary, a vessel of holy water. Care should be taken to make the occasion special and joyful.

Sick people who are unable to receive Communion under the form of bread may receive it under the form of wine alone. If the wine is consecrated at a Mass not celebrated in the presence of the sick person, the Blood of the Lord is kept in a properly covered vessel and is placed in the tabernacle after Communion. The Precious Blood should be carried to the sick in a vessel which is closed in such a way as to eliminate all danger of spilling. If some of the Precious Blood remains, it should be consumed by the minister, who should also see to it that the vessel is properly purified afterward by a Priest or Deacon.

75   If the sick wish to celebrate the Sacrament of Penance, it is preferable that the Priest make himself available for this during a previous visit.

76   If it is necessary to celebrate the Sacrament of Penance during the rite of Communion, it takes the place of the Penitential Act.

COMMUNION IN ORDINARY CIRCUMSTANCES

77   If possible, provision should be made to celebrate Mass in the homes of the sick, with their families and friends gathered around them. The Ordinary determines the conditions and requirements for such celebrations.

COMMUNION IN A HOSPITAL OR INSTITUTION

78   There will be situations, particularly in large institutions with many communicants, when the minister should consider alternative means so that the rite of Communion of the sick is not diminished to the absolute minimum. In such cases the following alternatives should be considered: (a) where possible, the residents or patients may be gathered in groups in one or more areas; (b) additional ministers of Communion may assist.
       When it is not possible to celebrate the full rite, the rite for Communion in a hospital or institution may be used. If it is convenient, however, the minister may add elements from the rite for ordinary circumstances, for example, a Scripture reading.

79   The rite begins with the recitation of the Eucharistic antiphon in the church, the hospital chapel, or the first room visited. Then the minister gives Communion to the sick in their individual rooms.

80   The concluding prayer may be said in the church, the hospital chapel, or the last room visited. No blessing is given.

COMMUNION IN ORDINARY CIRCUMSTANCES

INTRODUCTORY RITES

Greeting

81   The minister greets the sick person and the others present. One of the following may be used:

A

Peace be with this house and with all who live here.

B

The peace of the Lord be with you.

C

The grace of our Lord Jesus Christ
and the love of God
and the communion of the Holy Spirit be with you all.

D

Grace to you and peace from God our Father
and the Lord Jesus Christ.

If the minister is not a Priest or Deacon, he or she adds to the greeting:
Blessed be God for ever, *to which all respond:*

Blessed be God for ever.

The minister then places the Blessed Sacrament on the table and all join in adoration.

PENITENTIAL ACT

83   *The minister invites the sick person and all present to join in the Penitential Act, using these words:*

My brothers and sisters, to prepare ourselves for this celebration, let us call to mind our sins.

After a brief period of silence, the Penitential Act continues, using one of the following:

A

All say:
I confess to almighty God,
and to you, my brothers and sisters,
that I have greatly sinned,
in my thoughts and in my words,
in what I have done, and in what I have failed to do;

And, striking their breast, they say:
through my fault, through my fault,
through my most grievous fault;

Then they continue:
therefore I ask blessed Mary ever-virgin,
all the Angels and Saints,
and you, my brothers and sisters,
to pray for me to the Lord our God.

B

Have mercy on us, O Lord.
R. For we have sinned against you.
Show us, O Lord, your mercy.
R. And grant us your salvation.

C

By your Paschal Mystery
   you have won for us salvation:
Lord, have mercy.

R. Lord, have mercy.

You renew among us now
   the wonders of your Passion:
Christ, have mercy.

R. Christ, have mercy.

When we receive your Body
you share with us your Paschal sacrifice:
Lord, have mercy.

R. Lord, have mercy.

The minister concludes the Penitential Act with the following:
May almighty God have mercy on us,
forgive us our sins,
and bring us to everlasting life.

R. Amen.

LITURGY OF THE WORD

Reading

84   *The word of God is proclaimed by one of those present or by the minister. An appropriate reading from Part III or one of the following readings may be used:*

A John 6:51

B John 6:54–58

C John 14:6

D John 15:5

E 1 John 4:16

Response

85   *A brief period of silence may be observed after the reading of the word of God.*

The minister may then give a brief explanation of the reading, applying it to the needs of the sick person and those who are looking after him or her.

UNIVERSAL PRAYER

86   *The Universal Prayer (Prayer of the Faithful) may be said. With a brief introduction the minister invites all those present to pray. After the intentions the minister says the concluding prayer. It is desirable that the intentions be announced by someone other than the minister.*

Liturgy of Holy Communion

The Lord's Prayer

87 *The minister introduces the Lord's Prayer in these or similar words:*

A

Now let us pray as Christ the Lord has taught us:

B

And now let us pray with confidence as Christ our Lord commanded:

All say:

Our Father . . .

Communion

88 *The minister shows the Eucharistic Bread to those present, saying:*

Behold the Lamb of God,
behold him who takes away the sins of the world.
Blessed are those called to the supper of the Lamb.

The sick person and all who are to receive Communion say:

Lord, I am not worthy
that you should enter under my roof,
but only say the word
and my soul shall be healed.

The minister goes to the sick person and, showing the Blessed Sacrament, says:

The Body of Christ.

The sick person answers: Amen, *and receives Communion.*

Then if the Blood of Christ is to be given, the minister says:

The Blood of Christ.

The sick person answers: Amen, *and receives Communion. Others present who wish to receive Communion then do so in the usual way.*

Silent Prayer

89   *Then a period of silence may be observed.*

Prayer after Communion

90   *The minister says a concluding prayer. One of the following may be used:*

Let us pray.

Pause for silent prayer, if this has not preceded.

A

All-powerful and ever-living God,
may the Body and Blood of Christ your Son
be for our brother/sister **N.**
a lasting remedy for body and soul.
Through Christ our Lord.
R. *Amen.*

B

O God, who have accomplished the work of
        human redemption
through the Paschal Mystery of your Only Begotten Son,
graciously grant that we, who confidently proclaim,
under sacramental signs, the Death and Resurrection
        of Christ,
may experience continued increase of your saving grace.
Through Christ our Lord.
R. *Amen.*

C

O God, who willed that we be partakers
in the one Bread and the one Chalice,
grant us, we pray, so to live
that, made one in Christ,
we may joyfully bear fruit
for the salvation of the world.
Through Christ our Lord.

R. Amen.

D

Nourished by this sacred gift, O Lord,
we give you thanks and beseech your mercy,
that, by the pouring forth of your Spirit,
the grace of integrity may endure
in those your heavenly power has entered.
Through Christ our Lord.

R. Amen.

CONCLUDING RITE

Blessing

91   A minister who is not a Priest or Deacon invokes God's blessing and makes the Sign of the Cross on himself or herself, while saying:

A

May the Lord bless us,
protect us from all evil,
and bring us to everlasting life.

R. Amen.

B

May the almighty and merciful God bless and protect us,
the Father, and the Son, and the Holy Spirit.

R. Amen.

Communion in a Hospital or Institution

Introductory Rite

Antiphon

92   The rite may begin in the church, the hospital chapel, or the first room, where the minister says one of the following antiphons:

A

How holy this feast
in which Christ is our food:
his passion is recalled;
grace fills our hearts;
and we receive a pledge of the glory to come.

B

How gracious you are, Lord:
your gift of bread from heaven
reveals a Father's love and brings us perfect joy.
You fill the hungry with good things
and send the rich away empty.

C

I am the living bread
come down from heaven.
If you eat this bread
you will live for ever.
The bread I will give is my flesh
for the life of the world.

If it is customary, the minister may be accompanied by a person carrying a candle.

LITURGY OF HOLY COMMUNION

Greeting

93   *On entering each room, the minister may use one of the following greetings:*

A

The peace of the Lord be with you.

B

The grace of our Lord Jesus Christ
and the love of God
and the communion of the Holy Spirit be with you all.

If the minister is not a Priest or Deacon, he or she adds to the greeting:
Blessed be God for ever, *to which all respond:*

Blessed be God for ever.

The minister then places the Blessed Sacrament on the table, and all join in adoration.

If there is time and it seems desirable, the minister may proclaim a Scripture reading from those found in no. 84 or those appearing in Part III.

The Lord's Prayer

94   *When circumstances permit (for example, when there are not many rooms to visit), the minister is encouraged to lead the sick in the Lord's Prayer. The minister introduces the Lord's Prayer in these or similar words:*

A

Now let us pray as Christ the Lord has taught us:

B

And now let us pray with confidence as Christ our
Lord commanded:

All say:

Our Father . . .

Communion

95   *The minister shows the Eucharistic Bread to those present, saying:*

Behold the Lamb of God,
behold him who takes away the sins of the world.
Blessed are those called to the supper of the Lamb.

The sick person and all who are to receive Communion say:

Lord, I am not worthy
that you should enter under my roof,
but only say the word
and my soul shall be healed.

The minister goes to the sick person and, showing the Blessed Sacrament, says:
The Body of Christ.

The sick person answers: Amen, *and receives Communion.*

Then if the Blood of Christ is to be given, the minister says:
The Blood of Christ.

The sick person answers: Amen, *and receives Communion.*

Others present who wish to receive Communion then do so in the usual way.

CONCLUDING RITE

Concluding Prayer

96   The concluding prayer may be said either in the last room visited, in the church, or chapel. One of the following may be used:

Let us pray.

Pause for silent prayer, if this has not preceded.

A

All-powerful and ever-living God,
may the Body and Blood of Christ your Son
be for our brothers and sisters
a lasting remedy for body and soul.
Through Christ our Lord.

R. Amen.

B

O God, who have accomplished the work of human
      redemption
through the Paschal Mystery of your Only Begotten Son,
graciously grant that we, who confidently proclaim,
under sacramental signs, the Death and Resurrection
      of Christ,
may experience continued increase of your saving grace.
Through Christ our Lord.

R. Amen.

C

O God, who have willed that we be partakers
in the one Bread and the one Chalice,
grant us, we pray, so to live
that, made one in Christ,
we may joyfully bear fruit
for the salvation of the world.
Through Christ our Lord.

R. *Amen.*

D

Nourished by this sacred gift, O Lord,
we give you thanks and beseech your mercy,
that, by the pouring forth of your Spirit,
the grace of integrity may endure
in those your heavenly power has entered.
Through Christ our Lord.

R. *Amen.*

The blessing is omitted.

Pastoral Care of the Dying

INTRODUCTION

When we were baptized in Christ Jesus we were baptized into his death . . .
so that as Christ was raised from the dead by the Father's glory, we too
might live a new life.

161   The rites in Part II of *Pastoral Care of the Sick: Rites of Anointing and Viaticum* are used by the Church to comfort and strengthen a dying Christian in the passage from this life. The ministry to the dying places emphasis on trust in the Lord's promise of eternal life rather than on the struggle against illness which is characteristic of the pastoral care of the sick.

     The first three chapters of Part II provide for those situations in which time is not a pressing concern and the rites can be celebrated fully and properly. These are to be clearly distinguished from the rites contained in Chapter Eight, "Rites for Exceptional Circumstances," which provide for the emergency situations sometimes encountered in the ministry to the dying.

162   Priests with pastoral responsibilities are to direct the efforts of the family and friends as well as other ministers of the local Church in the care of the dying. They should ensure that all are familiar with the rites provided here.

     The words "Priest," "Deacon," and "minister" are used advisedly. Only in those rites which must be celebrated by a Priest is the word "Priest" used in the rubrics (that is, the Sacrament of Penance, the Sacrament of the Anointing of the Sick, the celebration of Viaticum within Mass). Whenever it is clear that, in the absence of a Priest, a Deacon may preside at a particular rite, the words "Priest or Deacon," are used in the rubrics. Whenever another minister is permitted to celebrate a rite in the absence of a Priest or Deacon, the word "minister" is used in the rubrics, even though in many cases the rite will be celebrated by a Priest or Deacon.

163   The Christian community has a continuing responsibility to pray for and with the person who is dying. Through its sacramental ministry to the dying the community helps Christians to embrace death in mysterious union with the crucified and risen Lord, who awaits them in the fullness of life.

CELEBRATION OF VIATICUM

164   A rite for Viaticum within Mass and another for Viaticum outside Mass are provided. If possible, and with the permission of the Ordinary, Viaticum should take place within the full Eucharistic celebration, with the family, friends, and other members of the Christian community taking part. The rite for Viaticum outside Mass is used when the full Eucharistic celebration cannot take place. Again, if it is possible, others should take part.

COMMENDATION OF THE DYING

165   The second chapter of Part II contains a collection of prayers for the spiritual comfort of the Christian who is close to death. These prayers are traditionally called the commendation of the dying to God and are to be used according to the circumstances of each case.

PRAYERS FOR THE DEAD

166   A chapter has also been provided to assist a minister who has been called to attend a person who is already dead. A Priest is not to administer the Sacrament of Anointing. Instead, he should pray for the dead person, using prayers such as those which appear in this chapter. He may find it necessary to explain to the family of the person who is dead that sacraments are celebrated for the living, not for the dead, and that the dead are effectively helped by the prayers of the living.

Rites for Exceptional Circumstances

167   Chapter Eight, "Rites for Exceptional Circumstances," contains rites which should be celebrated with a person who has suddenly been placed in proximate or immediate danger of death. They are for emergency circumstances and should be used only when such pressing conditions exist.

Care of a Dying Child

168   In its ministry to the dying the Church must also respond to the difficult circumstances of a dying child. Although no specific rites appear in Part II for the care of a dying child, these notes are provided to help bring into focus the various aspects of this ministry.

169   When parents learn that their child is dying, they are often bewildered and hurt. In their love for their son or daughter, they may be beset by temptations and doubts and find themselves asking: Why is God taking this child from us? How have we sinned or failed that God would punish us in this way? Why is this innocent child being hurt?

Under these trying circumstances, much of the Church's ministry will be directed to the parents and family. While pain and suffering in an innocent child are difficult for others to bear, the Church helps the parents and family to accept what God has allowed to happen. It should be understood by all beforehand that this process of acceptance will probably extend beyond the death of the child. The concern of the Christian community should continue as long as necessary.

Concern for the child must be equal to that for the family. Those who deal with dying children observe that their faith matures rapidly. Though young children often seem to accept death more easily than adults, they will often experience a surprisingly mature anguish because of the pain which they see in their families.

170   At such a time, it is important for members of the Christian community to come to the support of the child and the family by prayer, visits, and other forms of assistance. Those who have lost children of their own have a ministry of consolation and support to the family. Hospital personnel (doctors, nurses, aides) should also be prepared to exercise a special role with the child as caring adults. Priests and Deacons bear particular responsibility for overseeing all these elements of the Church's pastoral ministry. The minister should invite members of the community to use their individual gifts in this work of communal care and concern.

171   By conversation and brief services of readings and prayers, the minister may help the parents and family to see that their child is being called ahead of them to enter the kingdom and joy of the Lord. The period when the child is dying can become a special time of renewal and prayer for the family and close friends. The minister should help them to see that the child's sufferings are united to those of Jesus for the salvation of the whole world.

172   If it is appropriate, the Priest should discuss with the parents the possibility of preparing and celebrating with the child the Sacraments of Initiation (Baptism, Confirmation, Eucharist). The Priest may baptize and confirm the child (see *Rite of Confirmation,* no. 7b). To complete the process of Initiation, the child should also receive first Communion.

According to the circumstances, some of these rites may be celebrated by a Deacon or layperson. So that the child and family may receive full benefit from them, these rites are normally celebrated over a period of time. In this case, the minister should use the usual rites, that is, the *Rite of Baptism for Children,* the *Rite of Confirmation,* and if suitable, the *Rite of Penance.* Similarly, if time allows, the usual rites for Anointing and Viaticum should be celebrated.

173   If sudden illness or an accident has placed an uninitiated child in proximate danger of death, the minister uses "Christian Initiation for the Dying," adapting it for use with a child.

174   For an initiated child or a child lacking only the Sacrament of Confirmation, who is in proximate danger of death, the "Continuous Rite of Penance, Anointing, and Viaticum" may be used and adapted to the understanding of the child. If death is imminent it should be remembered that Viaticum rather than Anointing is the sacrament for the dying.

Celebration of Viaticum

INTRODUCTION

I am going to prepare a place for you; I shall come back and take you with me.

175   This chapter contains a rite for Viaticum within Mass and a rite for Viaticum outside Mass. The celebration of the Eucharist as Viaticum, food for the passage through death to eternal life, is the sacrament proper to the dying Christian. It is the completion and crown of the Christian life on this earth, signifying that the Christian follows the Lord to eternal glory and the banquet of the heavenly kingdom.

     The Sacrament of the Anointing of the Sick should be celebrated at the beginning of a serious illness. Viaticum, celebrated when death is close, will then be better understood as the last sacrament of Christian life.

176   Priests and other ministers entrusted with the spiritual care of the sick should do everything they can to ensure that those in proximate danger of death receive the Body and Blood of Christ as Viaticum. At the earliest opportunity, the necessary preparation should be given to the dying person, family, and others who may take part.

177   Whenever it is possible, the dying Christian should be able to receive Viaticum within Mass. In this way he or she shares fully, during the final moments of this life, in the Eucharistic Sacrifice, which proclaims the Lord's own passing through death to life. However, circumstances, such as confinement to a hospital ward or the very emergency which makes death imminent, may frequently make the complete Eucharistic celebration impossible. In this case, the rite for Viaticum outside Mass is appropriate. The minister should wear attire appropriate to this ministry.

178   Because the celebration of Viaticum ordinarily takes place in the limited circumstances of the home, a hospital, or other institution,

the simplifications of the rite for Masses in small gatherings may be appropriate. Depending on the condition of the dying person, every effort should be made to involve him or her, the family, friends, and other members of the local community in the planning and celebration. Appropriate readings, prayers, and songs will help to foster the full participation of all. Because of this concern for participation, the minister should ensure that Viaticum is celebrated while the dying person is still able to take part and respond.

179   A distinctive feature of the celebration of Viaticum, whether within or outside Mass, is the renewal of the baptismal profession of faith by the dying person. This occurs after the Homily and replaces the usual form of the Profession of Faith. Through the baptismal profession at the end of earthly life, the one who is dying uses the language of his or her initial commitment, which is renewed each Easter and on other occasions in the Christian life. In the context of Viaticum, it is a renewal and fulfillment of initiation into the Christian mysteries, Baptism leading to the Eucharist.

180   The rites for Viaticum within and outside Mass may include the sign of peace. The minister and all who are present embrace the dying Christian. In this and in other parts of the celebration the sense of leave-taking need not be concealed or denied, but the joy of Christian hope, which is the comfort and strength of the one near death, should also be evident.

181   As an indication that the reception of the Eucharist by the dying Christian is a pledge of resurrection and food for the passage through death, the special words proper to Viaticum are added: "May the Lord Jesus Christ protect you and lead you to eternal life." The dying person and all who are present may receive Communion under both kinds. The sign of Communion is more complete when received in this manner because it expresses more fully and clearly the nature of the Eucharist as a meal, one which prepares all who take part in it for the heavenly banquet (see the *General Instruction of the Roman Missal,* no. 281).

        The minister should choose the manner of giving Communion under both kinds which is suitable in the particular case. If the wine is consecrated at a Mass not celebrated in the presence of the sick person, the Blood of the Lord is kept in a properly covered vessel and is placed in the tabernacle after Communion. The Precious Blood should be carried to the sick person in a vessel which is closed in such a way as to eliminate all danger of spilling. If some of the Precious Blood remains after Communion, it should be consumed by the minister, who should also see to it that the vessel is properly purified afterward by a Priest or Deacon.

The sick who are unable to receive under the form of bread may receive under the form of wine alone. If the wine is consecrated at a Mass not celebrated in the presence of the sick person, the instructions given above are followed.

182   In addition to these elements of the rites which are to be given greater stress, special texts are provided for the Universal Prayer or litany and the final Solemn Blessing.

183   It often happens that a person who has received the Eucharist as Viaticum lingers in a grave condition or at the point of death for a period of days or longer. In these circumstances he or she should be given the opportunity to receive the Eucharist as Viaticum on successive days, frequently if not daily. This may take place during or outside Mass as particular conditions permit. The rite may be simplified according to the condition of the one who is dying.

VIATICUM WITHIN MASS

184   When Viaticum is received within Mass, the ritual Mass for Viaticum or the Mass of the Holy Eucharist may be celebrated. The priest wears white vestments. The readings may be taken from the *Lectionary for Mass* (second edition, nos. 796–800), unless the dying person and those involved with the Priest in planning the liturgy choose other readings from Scripture.

A ritual Mass is not permitted during the Easter Triduum, on the Solemnities of Christmas, Epiphany, Ascension, Pentecost, Corpus Christi, or on a Solemnity which is a Holyday of Obligation. On these occasions, the texts and readings are taken from the Mass of the day. Although the Mass for Viaticum or the Mass of the Holy Eucharist are also excluded on the Sundays of Advent, Lent, and Easter Time, on Solemnities, Ash Wednesday, and the weekdays of Holy Week, one of the readings may be taken from the biblical texts indicated above. The special form of the final blessing may be used and, at the discretion of the Priest, the Apostolic Pardon may be added.

185 If the dying person wishes to celebrate the Sacrament of Penance, it is preferable that the Priest make himself available for this during a previous visit. If this is not possible, the Sacrament of Penance may be celebrated before Mass begins (see Appendix, p. 372).

VIATICUM OUTSIDE MASS

186 Although Viaticum celebrated in the context of the full Eucharistic celebration is always preferable, when it is not possible the rite for Viaticum outside Mass is appropriate. This rite includes some of the elements of the Mass, especially a brief Liturgy of the Word. Depending on the circumstances and the condition of the dying person, this rite should also be a communal celebration. Every effort should be made to involve the dying person, family, friends, and members of the local community in the planning and celebration. The manner of celebration and the elements of the rite which are used should be accommodated to those present and the nearness of death.

187 If the dying person wishes to celebrate the Sacrament of Penance and this cannot take place during a previous visit, it should be celebrated before the rite of Viaticum begins, especially if others are present. Alternatively, it may be celebrated during the rite of Viaticum, replacing the Penitential Act. At the discretion of the Priest, the Apostolic Pardon may be added after the Penitential Act or after the Sacrament of Penance.

188 An abbreviated Liturgy of the Word, ordinarily consisting of a single biblical reading, gives the minister an opportunity to explain the word of God in relation to Viaticum. The sacrament should be described as the sacred food which strengthens the Christian for the passage through death to life in sure hope of the resurrection.

Viaticum outside Mass

Introductory Rites

Greeting

197   The minister greets the sick person and the others present. The following may be used:

A

Peace be with this house and with all who live here.

B

The peace of the Lord be with you.

C

The grace of our Lord Jesus Christ
and the love of God
and the communion of the Holy Spirit be with you all.

D

Grace to you and peace from God our Father
and the Lord Jesus Christ.

*If the minister is not a Priest or Deacon, he or she adds to the greeting:
Blessed be God for ever, to which all respond:*

Blessed be God for ever.

The minister then places the Blessed Sacrament on the table, and all join in adoration.

Instruction

199   Afterward the minister addresses those present, using the following instruction or one better suited to the sick person's condition:

My brothers and sisters, before our Lord Jesus Christ passed from this world to return to the Father, he left us the sacrament of his Body and Blood. When the hour comes for us to pass from this life and join him, he strengthens us with this food for our journey and comforts us by this pledge of our resurrection.

Penitential Act

200   The minister invites the sick person and all present to join in the Penitential Act, using these words:

My brothers and sisters, to prepare ourselves for this celebration, let us call to mind our sins.

After a brief period of silence, the Penitential Act continues using one of the following prayers.

A   *All say:*

I confess to almighty God,
and to you, my brothers and sisters,
that I have greatly sinned,
in my thoughts and in my words,
in what I have done, and in what I have failed to do;

And, striking thier breast, they say:

through my fault, through my fault,
through my most grievous fault;

Then they continue:

therefore I ask blessed Mary ever-virgin,
all the Angels and Saints,
and you, my brothers and sisters,
to pray for me to the Lord our God.

B

By your Paschal Mystery
   you have won for us salvation:
Lord, have mercy.
***R.** Lord, have mercy.*

You renew among us now
   the wonders of your Passion:
Christ, have mercy.
***R.** Christ, have mercy.*

When we receive your Body,
you share with us your Paschal sacrifice:
Lord, have mercy.
***R.** Lord, have mercy.*

The minister concludes the Penitential Act with the following:
May almighty God have mercy us,
forgive us our sins,
and bring us to everlasting life.
***R.** Amen.*

LITURGY OF THE WORD

Reading

202   The word of God is proclaimed by one of those present or by the minister. An appropriate reading from Part III or one of the following may be used:

A John 6:54–55

B John 14:23

C John 15:4

D 1 Corinthians 11:26

Homily

203   Depending on circumstances, the minister may then give a brief explanation of the reading.

Baptismal Profession of Faith

204   It is desirable that the sick person renew his or her baptismal profession of faith before receiving Viaticum. The minister gives a brief introduction and then asks the following questions:

N., do you believe in God,
the Father almighty,
Creator of heaven and earth?

R. *I do.*

Do you believe in Jesus Christ, his only Son, our Lord,
who was born of the Virgin Mary,
suffered death and was buried,
rose again from the dead
and is seated at the right hand of the Father?

R. *I do.*

Do you believe in the Holy Spirit,
the holy Catholic Church,
the communion of saints,
the forgiveness of sins,
the resurrection of the body,
and life everlasting?

R. *I do.*

Litany

205 The minister may adapt or shorten the litany according to the condition of the sick person. The litany may be omitted if the sick person has made the Profession of Faith and appears to be tiring.

My brothers and sisters, with one heart let us call on our Savior Jesus Christ.

You loved us to the very end and gave yourself over to death in order to give us life. For our brother/sister, Lord, we pray:

R. *Lord, hear our prayer.*

You said to us: "All who eat my flesh and drink my blood will live for ever." For our brother/sister, Lord, we pray:

R. *Lord, hear our prayer.*

You invite us to join in the banquet where pain and sorrow, sadness and separation will be no more. For our brother/sister, Lord, we pray:

R. *Lord, hear our prayer.*

LITURGY OF VIATICUM

The Lord's Prayer

206   The minister introduces the Lord's Prayer in these words:

A

Now let us offer together the prayer our Lord Jesus Christ taught us:

B

And now let us pray with confidence as Christ our Lord commanded:

All say:

Our Father . . .

Communion as Viaticum

207   The sick person and all present may receive Communion under both kinds. When the minister gives Communion to the sick person, the form for Viaticum is used.

The minister shows the Eucharistic Bread to those present, saying:

Behold the Lamb of God,
behold him who takes away the sins of the world.
Blessed are those called to the supper of the Lamb.

The sick person and all who are to receive Communion say:

Lord, I am not worthy
that you should enter under my roof,
but only say the word
and my soul shall be healed.

The minister goes to the sick person and, showing the Blessed Sacrament, says:

The Body of Christ.

The sick person answers: Amen.
Then if the Blood of Christ is to be given, the minister says:

The Blood of Christ.

The sick person answers: Amen.

Immediately, or after giving Communion to the sick person, the minister adds:

May the Lord Jesus Christ protect you and lead you to eternal life.

R. Amen.

Others present who wish to receive Communion then do so in the usual way.

After the conclusion of the rite, the minister cleanses the vessel as usual.

Silent Prayer
208   Then a period of silence may be observed.

Prayer after Communion
209   The minister says the concluding prayer.

Let us pray.

Pause for silent prayer, if this has not preceded.

A

O God, whose Son is for us the way, the truth and the life,
look lovingly upon your servant **N.**
and grant that, trusting in your promises
and strengthened by the Body of your Son,
he (she) may journey in peace to your Kingdom.
Through Christ our Lord.

R. *Amen.*

B

O Lord, eternal health and salvation
of those who believe in you,
grant, we pray, that your servant *N.*,
renewed by heavenly food and drink,
may safely reach your Kingdom of light and life.
Through Christ our Lord.

R. *Amen.*

C

All-powerful and ever-living God,
may the Body and Blood of Christ your Son
be for our brother/sister *N.*
a lasting remedy for body and soul.

Through Christ our Lord.
R. *Amen.*

CONCLUDING RITES

Blessing

210   A minister who is not a Priest or Deacon invokes God's blessing and makes the Sign of the Cross on himself or herself, while saying:

A

May the Lord bless us,
protect us from all evil,
and bring us to everlasting life.
R. *Amen.*

B

May the almighty and merciful God bless and protect us,
the Father, and the Son, and the Holy Spirit.
R. *Amen.*

Sign of Peace

211   The minister and the others present may then give the sick person the sign of peace.

Commendation
of the Dying

INTRODUCTION

Into your hands, Lord, I commend my spirit.

212   In Viaticum the dying person is united with Christ in his passage out of this world to the Father. Through the prayers for the commendation of the dying contained in this chapter, the Church helps to sustain this union until it is brought to fulfillment after death.

213   Christians have the responsibility of expressing their union in Christ by joining the dying person in prayer for God's mercy and for confidence in Christ. In particular, the presence of a Priest or Deacon shows more clearly that the Christian dies in the communion of the Church. He should assist the dying person and those present in the recitation of the prayers of commendation and, following death, he should lead those present in the prayer after death. If the Priest or Deacon is unable to be present because of other serious pastoral obligations, other members of the community should be prepared to assist with these prayers and should have the texts readily available to them.

214   The minister may choose texts from among the prayers, litanies, aspirations, psalms, and readings provided in this chapter, or others may be added. In the selection of these texts the minister should keep in mind the condition and piety of both the dying person and the members of the family who are present. The prayers are best said in a slow, quiet voice, alternating with periods of silence. If possible, the minister says one or more of the brief prayer formulas with the dying person. These may be softly repeated two or three times.

215   These texts are intended to help the dying person, if still conscious, to face the natural human anxiety about death by imitating

Christ in his patient suffering and dying. The Christian will be helped to surmount his or her fear in the hope of heavenly life and resurrection through the power of Christ, who destroyed the power of death by his own dying.

Even if the dying person is not conscious, those who are present will draw consolation from these prayers and come to a better understanding of the paschal character of Christian death. This may be visibly expressed by making the Sign of the Cross on the forehead of the dying person, who was first signed with the cross at Baptism.

216   Immediately after death has occurred, all may kneel while one of those present leads the prayers given on nos. 221–222.

SHORT TEXTS

217   One or more of the following short texts may be recited with the dying person. If necessary, they may be softly repeated two or three times.

Romans 8:35
Who can separate us from the love of Christ?

Romans 14:8
Whether we live or die, we are the Lord's.

2 Corinthians 5:1
We have an everlasting home in heaven.

1 Thessalonians 4:17
We shall be with the Lord for ever.

1 John 3:2
We shall see God as he really is.

1 John 3:14
We have passed from death to life
because we love each other.

Psalm 25:1
To you, Lord, I lift up my soul.

Psalm 27:1
The Lord is my light and my salvation.

Psalm 27:13
I believe that I shall see the goodness of the Lord
in the land of the living.

Psalm 42:3
My soul thirsts for the living God.

Psalm 23:4
Though I walk in the shadow of death,
I will fear no evil, for you are with me.

Matthew 25:34
Come, blessed of my Father,
says the Lord Jesus,
and take possession of the kingdom
prepared for you.

Luke 23:43
The Lord Jesus says,
today you will be with me in paradise.

John 14:2
In my Father's home
there are many dwelling places,
says the Lord Jesus.

John 14:2–3
The Lord Jesus says,
I go to prepare a place for you,
and I will come again to take you to myself.

John 17:24
I desire that where I am,
they also may be with me,
says the Lord Jesus.

John 6:40
Everyone who believes in the Son
has eternal life.

Psalm 31:6a
Into your hands, Lord,
I commend my spirit.

Acts 7:59
Lord Jesus, receive my spirit.

Holy Mary, pray for me.

Saint Joseph, pray for me.

Jesus, Mary, and Joseph,
assist me in my last agony.

Reading

218   *The word of God is proclaimed by one of those present or by the minister. Selections from Part III or from the following readings may be used:*

A. *Job 19:23–27*
Job's act of faith is a model for our own; God is the God of the living.

B. *Psalm 23*

C. *Psalm 25*

D. *Psalm 91*

E. *Psalm 121*

F. *1 John 4:16*

G. *Revelation 21:1–5a, 6–7*
God our Father is the God of newness of life; it is his desire that we should come to share his life with him.

H. *Matthew 25:1–13*
Jesus bid us be prepared for our ultimate destiny, which is eternal life.

I. *Luke 22:39–46*
Jesus is alive to our pain and sorrow, because faithfulness to his Father's will cost him life itself.

J. *Luke 23:44–49*
Jesus' death is witnessed by his friends.

K. Luke 24:1–8
Jesus is alive; he gives us eternal life with the Father.

L. John 6:37–40
Jesus will raise his own from death and give them eternal life.

M. John 14:1–6, 23, 27
The love of Jesus can raise us up from the sorrow of death to the joy of eternal life.

Litany of the Saints

219   When the condition of the dying person calls for the use of brief forms of prayer, those who are present are encouraged to pray the Litany of the Saints—or at least some of its invocations—for him or her. Special mention may be made of the Patron Saints of the dying person, of the family, and of the parish. The Litany may be said or sung in the usual way. Other customary prayers may also be used.

A

Lord, have mercy	*Lord, have mercy*
Christ, have mercy	*Christ, have mercy*
Lord, have mercy	*Lord, have mercy*
Holy Mary, Mother of God	*pray for him/her*
Holy Angels of God	*pray for him/her*
Abraham, our father in faith	*pray for him/her*
David, leader of God's people	*pray for him/her*
All holy patriarchs and prophets	*pray for him/her*
Saint John the Baptist	*pray for him/her*
Saint Joseph	*pray for him/her*
Saint Peter and Saint Paul	*pray for him/her*
Saint Andrew	*pray for him/her*
Saint John	*pray for him/her*
Saint Mary Magdalene	*pray for him/her*

Saint Stephen. . . . . *pray for him/her*

Saint Ignatius . . . . *pray for him/her*

Saint Lawrence . . . . *pray for him/her*

Saint Perpetua and Saint Felicity . . . . *pray for him/her*

Saint Agnes . . . . *pray for him/her*

Saint Gregory . . . . *pray for him/her*

Saint Augustine . . . . *pray for him/her*

Saint Athanasius. . . . . *pray for him/her*

Saint Basil . . . . *pray for him/her*

Saint Martin . . . . *pray for him/her*

Saint Benedict. . . . . *pray for him/her*

Saint Francis and Saint Dominic . . . . *pray for him/her*

Saint Francis Xavier . . . . *pray for him/her*

Saint John Vianney . . . . *pray for him/her*

Saint Catherine. . . . . *pray for him/her*

Saint Teresa . . . . *pray for him/her*

Other Saints may be included here.

All holy men and women. . . . . *pray for him/her*

Lord, be merciful . . . . *Lord, save your people*

From all evil . . . . *Lord, save your people*

From every sin . . . . *Lord, save your people*

From Satan's power . . . . *Lord, save your people*

At the moment of death. . . . . *Lord, save your people*

From everlasting death . . . . *Lord, save your people*

On the day of judgment. . . . . *Lord, save your people*

By your coming as man . . . . *Lord, save your people*

By your suffering and Cross . . . . *Lord, save your people*

By your Death
          and rising to new life . . . . *Lord, save your people*

By your return in glory
      to the Father . . . . *Lord, save your people*

By your gift
      of the Holy Spirit . . . . *Lord, save your people*

By your coming again
      in glory. . . . . *Lord, save your people*

Be merciful to us sinners . . . . *Lord, hear our prayer*

Bring *N.* to eternal life,
      first promised to
      him/her in Baptism . . . . *Lord, hear our prayer*

Raise *N.* on the last day,
      for he/she has eaten
      the Bread of life. . . . . *Lord, hear our prayer*

Let *N.* share in your glory,
      for he/she has shared
      in your suffering
      and Death . . . . *Lord, hear our prayer*

Jesus, Son of the living God. . . . . *Lord, hear our prayer*

Christ, hear us. . . . . *Christ, hear us*

Lord Jesus, hear our prayer . . . . *Lord, hear our prayer*

B

A brief form of the Litany may be prayed. Other Saints may be added, including the Patron Saints of the dying person, of the family, and of the parish; Saints to whom the dying person may have a special devotion may also be included.

Holy Mary, Mother of God . . . . *pray for him/her*

Holy Angels of God . . . . *pray for him/her*

Saint John the Baptist. . . . . *pray for him/her*

Saint Joseph. . . . . *pray for him/her*

Saint Peter and Saint Paul . . . . *pray for him/her*

Other Saints may be included here.

All holy men and women . . . . *pray for him/her*

Prayer of Commendation

220   When the moment of death seems near, some of the following prayers may be said:

A

Go forth, Christian soul, from this world
in the name of God the almighty Father,
who created you,
in the name of Jesus Christ, Son of the living God,
who suffered for you,
in the name of the Holy Spirit,
who was poured out upon you,
go forth, faithful Christian.

May you live in peace this day,
may your home be with God in Zion,
with Mary, the virgin Mother of God,
with Joseph, and all the Angels and Saints.

B

I commend you, my dear brother/sister,
to almighty God,
and entrust you to your Creator.
May you return to him
who formed you from the dust of the earth.
May holy Mary, the Angels, and all the Saints
come to meet you as you go forth from this life.

May Christ who was crucified for you
bring you freedom and peace.
May Christ who died for you
admit you into his garden of paradise.
May Christ, the true Shepherd,
acknowledge you as one of his flock.
May he forgive all your sins,
and set you among those he has chosen.
May you see your Redeemer face to face,
and enjoy the vision of God for ever.

R. Amen.

C

Welcome your servant, Lord, into the place of salvation which
because of your mercy he/she rightly hoped for.

R. Amen, or *R. Lord, save your people.*

Deliver your servant, Lord, from every distress.

R. Amen, or *R. Lord, save your people.*

Deliver your servant, Lord, as you delivered Noah
from the flood.

R. Amen, or *R. Lord, save your people.*

Deliver your servant, Lord, as you delivered Abraham from
Ur of the Chaldees.

R. Amen, or *R. Lord, save your people.*

Deliver your servant, Lord, as you delivered Moses
from the hand of the Pharaoh.

R. Amen, or *R. Lord, save your people.*

Deliver your servant, Lord, as you delivered Daniel
from the den of lions.

R. *Amen,* or **R.** *Lord, save your people.*

Deliver your servant, Lord, as you delivered the three young
men from the fiery furnace.

R. *Amen,* or **R.** *Lord, save your people.*

Deliver your servant, Lord, as you delivered Susanna
from her false accusers.

R. *Amen,* or **R.** *Lord, save your people.*

Deliver your servant, Lord, as you delivered David
from the attacks of Saul and Goliath.

R. *Amen,* or **R.** *Lord, save your people.*

Deliver your servant, Lord, as you delivered Peter and Paul
from prison.

R. *Amen,* or **R.** *Lord, save your people.*

Deliver your servant, Lord, through Jesus our Savior,
who suffered death for us and gave us eternal life.

R. *Amen,* or **R.** *Lord, save your people.*

D

Lord Jesus Christ, Savior of the world,
we pray for your servant **N.**,
and commend him/her to your mercy.
For his/her sake you came down from heaven;
receive him/her now into the joy of your kingdom.

For though he/she has sinned,
he/she has not denied the Father, the Son, and the Holy Spirit,
but has believed in God
and has worshipped his/her Creator.
R. *Amen.*

E   *The following antiphon may be said or sung:*

Hail, holy Queen, Mother of mercy,
hail, our life, our sweetness, and our hope.
To you we cry, the children of Eve;
to you we send up our sighs,
mourning and weeping in this land of exile.
Turn, then, most gracious advocate,
your eyes of mercy toward us;
lead us home at last
and show us the blessed fruit of your womb, Jesus:
O clement, O loving, O sweet Virgin Mary.

Prayer after Death

221 When death has occurred, one or more of the following prayers may be said:

A

Saints of God, come to his/her aid!
Come to meet him/her, Angels of the Lord!

R. *Receive his/her soul and present him/her to God the Most High.*

May Christ, who called you, take you to himself;
may Angels lead you to Abraham's side.

R. *Receive his/her soul and present him/her to God the Most High.*

Give him/her eternal rest, O Lord,
and may your light shine on him/her for ever.

R. *Receive his/her soul and present him/her to God the Most High.*

The following prayer is added:
Let us pray.

All-powerful and merciful God,
we commend to you **N.**, your servant.
In your mercy and love,
blot out the sins he/she has committed
    through human weakness.
In this world he/she has died:
let him/her live with you for ever.
Through Christ our Lord.

R. *Amen.*

For the solace of those present the minister may conclude these prayers with a simple blessing or with a symbolic gesture, for example, signing the forehead with the Sign of the Cross.

B PSALM 130

R. My soul hopes in the Lord.

Out of the depths I cry to you, O LORD;
  LORD, hear my voice!
Let your ears be attentive
  to my voice in supplication. *R.*

I trust in the LORD,
  my soul trusts in his word.
My soul waits for the LORD
  more than sentinels wait for the dawn. *R.*

For with the LORD is kindness,
  and with him is plenteous redemption.
And he will redeem Israel
  from all their iniquities. *R.*

The following prayer is added:
Let us pray.
God of love,
welcome into your presence
your son/daughter **N.**, whom you have
    called from this life.
Release him/her from all his/her sins,
bless him/her with eternal light and peace,
raise him/her up to live for ever with all your Saints
in the glory of the resurrection.

Through Christ our Lord.
R. *Amen.*

C   PSALM 23

R. *Lord, remember me in your kingdom.*

The LORD is my shepherd; I shall not want.
    In verdant pastures he gives me repose;
Beside restful waters he leads me;
    he refreshes my soul. **R.**

He guides me in right paths
    for his name's sake.
Even though I walk in the dark valley
    I fear no evil; for you are at my side
With your rod and your staff
    that give me courage. **R.**

You spread the table before me
    in the sight of my foes;
You anoint my head with oil;
    my cup overflows. **R.**

Only goodness and kindness follow me
    all the days of my life;
And I shall dwell in the house of the Lord
    for years to come. **R.**

The following prayer is added:
Let us pray.
God of mercy,
hear our prayers and be merciful
to your son/daughter **N.**,
    whom you have called from this life.
Welcome him/her into the company of your Saints,
in the kingdom of light and peace.

Through Christ our Lord.
R. *Amen.*

D

Almighty and eternal God,
hear our prayers for your son/daughter **N.**,
whom you have called from this life to yourself.
Grant him/her light, happiness, and peace.
Let him/her pass in safety through the gates
of death,
and live for ever with all your Saints
in the light you promised to Abraham
and to all his descendants in faith.

Guard him/her from all harm
and on that great day of resurrection and reward
raise him/her up with all your Saints.
Pardon his/her sins
and give him/her eternal life in your kingdom.

Through Christ our Lord.
R. *Amen.*

E

Loving and merciful God,
we entrust our brother/sister to your mercy.
You loved him/her greatly in this life:
now that he/she is freed from all its cares,
give him/her happiness and peace for ever.

The old order has passed away:
welcome him/her now into paradise
where there will be no more sorrow,
no more weeping or pain,

but only peace and joy
with Jesus, your Son,
and the Holy Spirit
for ever and ever.
R. Amen.

F

God of our destiny,
into your hands we commend our brother/sister.
We are confident that with all who have died in Christ
he/she will be raised to life on the last day
and live with Christ for ever.

[We thank you for all the blessings
you gave him/her in this life
to show your fatherly care for all of us
and the fellowship which is ours with the Saints in Jesus Christ.]

Lord, hear our prayer:
welcome our brother/sister to paradise
and help us to comfort each other
with the assurance of our faith
until we all meet in Christ
to be with you and with our brother/sister for ever.

Through Christ our Lord.
R. Amen.

Prayer for the Family and Friends

222 *The following prayer may be said:*

Let us pray.

A *For the family and friends*

God of all consolation,
in your unending love and mercy for us
you turn the darkness of death
into the dawn of new life.
Show compassion to your people in their sorrow.
[Be our refuge and our strength
to lift us from the darkness of this grief
to the peace and light of your presence.]
Your Son, our Lord Jesus Christ,
by dying for us, conquered death
and by rising again, restored life.
May we then go forward eagerly to meet him,
and after our life on earth
be reunited with our brothers and sisters
where every tear will be wiped away.
Through Christ our Lord.

R. *Amen.*

B   *For the deceased person and for family and friends*

Lord Jesus, our Redeemer,
you willingly gave yourself up to death
so that all people might be saved
and pass from death into new life.
Listen to our prayers,
look with love on your people
who mourn and pray for their brother/sister **N.**

Lord Jesus, holy and compassionate:
forgive **N.** his/her sins.
By dying you opened the gates of life
for those who believe in you:
do not let our brother/sister be parted from you,
but by your glorious power
give him/her light, joy, and peace in heaven
where you live for ever and ever.
R. *Amen.*

For the solace of those present the minister may conclude these prayers
with a simple blessing or with a symbolic gesture, for example, signing the
forehead with the Sign of the Cross.

Prayers for the Dead

INTRODUCTION

I want those you have given me to be with me where I am.

223   This chapter contains prayers for use by a minister who has been called to attend a person who is already dead. A Priest is not to administer the Sacraments of Penance or Anointing. Instead, he should pray for the dead person using these or similar prayers.

224   It may be necessary to explain to the family of the person who is dead that sacraments are celebrated for the living, not for the dead, and that the dead are effectively helped by the prayers of the living.

225   To comfort those present the minister may conclude these prayers with a simple blessing or with a symbolic gesture, for example, making the Sign of the Cross on the forehead. A Priest or Deacon may sprinkle the body with holy water.

Greeting
226   The minister greets those who are present, offering them sympathy and the consolation of faith, using the following or similar words:

A

In this moment of sorrow
the Lord is in our midst
and comforts us with his word:
Blessed are the sorrowful; they shall be consoled.

B

Praised be God, the Father of our Lord Jesus Christ,
the Father of mercies,
and the God of all consolation!
He comforts us in all our afflictions
and thus enables us to comfort those who are in trouble,
with the same consolation
we have received from him.

Prayer

227   *The minister then says one of the following prayers, commending
the person who has just died to God's mercy and goodness:*

Let us pray.

A

Almighty and eternal God,
hear our prayers for your son/daughter **N.**,
whom you have called from this life to yourself.

Grant him/her light, happiness, and peace.
Let him/her pass in safety through the gates of death,
and live for ever with all your Saints
in the light you promised to Abraham
and to all his descendants in faith.

Guard him/her from all harm
and on that great day of resurrection and reward
raise him/her up with all your Saints.
Pardon his/her sins
and give him/her eternal life in your kingdom.

Through Christ our Lord.
R. Amen.

B

Loving and merciful God,
we entrust our brother/sister to your mercy.
You loved him/her greatly in this life:
now that he/she is freed from all its cares,
give him/her happiness and peace for ever.

The old order has passed away:
welcome him/her now into paradise
where there will be no more sorrow,
no more weeping or pain,
but only peace and joy
with Jesus, your Son,
and the Holy Spirit
for ever and ever.

R. *Amen.*

Reading

228   The word of God is proclaimed by one of those present or by the minister. One of the following readings may be used:

A Luke 23:44–46
B John 11:3–7, 20–27, 33–36, 41–44

Litany

229 Then one of those present may lead the others in praying a brief form of the Litany of the Saints. (The full form of the Litany of the Saints may be found in no. 219.) Other Saints may be added, including the Patron Saints of the dead person, of the family, and of the parish; Saints to whom the deceased person may have had a special devotion may also be included.

Saints of God, come to his/her aid!
Come to meet him/her, Angels of the Lord!

Holy Mary, Mother of God . . . .*pray for him/her*
Saint Joseph. . . . .*pray for him/her*
Saint Peter and Saint Paul . . . .*pray for him/her*
The following prayer is added:

God of mercy,
hear our prayers and be merciful
to your son/daughter **N.**, whom you have called from this life.
Welcome him/her into the company of your Saints,
in the kingdom of light and peace.

Through Christ our Lord.
R. *Amen.*

The Lord's Prayer
230 The minister introduces the Lord's Prayer in these or similar words:

A

With God there is mercy and fullness of redemption; let us pray as Jesus taught us to pray:

B

Let us pray for the coming of the kingdom as Jesus taught us:
All say:

Our Father . . .

Prayer of Commendation

231   The minister then concludes with the following prayer:

Lord Jesus, our Redeemer,
you willingly gave yourself up to death
so that all people might be saved
and pass from death into a new life.
Listen to our prayers,
look with love on your people
who mourn and pray for their brother/sister **N.**

Lord Jesus, holy and compassionate:
forgive **N.** his/her sins.
By dying you opened the gates of life
for those who believe in you:
do not let our brother/sister be parted from you,
but by your glorious power
give him/her light, joy, and peace in heaven
where you live for ever and ever.

R. *Amen.*

*For the solace of those present the minister may conclude these prayers
with a simple blessing or with a symbolic gesture, for example, signing the
forehead with the Sign of the Cross.*

THE GOSPEL AND EXPLANATIONS OF THE READING

ADVENT

December 2, 2018

FIRST SUNDAY OF ADVENT

**A reading from the holy Gospel
according to Luke** 21:25–28, 34–36

Jesus said to his disciples:
"There will be signs in the sun, the moon,
    and the stars,
    and on earth nations will be in dismay,
    perplexed by the roaring of the sea and the waves.
People will die of fright
    in anticipation of what is coming upon the world,
    for the powers of the heavens will be shaken.
And then they will see the Son of Man
    coming in a cloud with power and great glory.
But when these signs begin to happen,
    stand erect and raise your heads
    because your redemption is at hand.

"Beware that your hearts do not become drowsy
    from carousing and drunkenness
    and the anxieties of daily life,
    and that day catch you by surprise like a trap.
For that day will assault everyone
    who lives on the face of the earth.

Be vigilant at all times
    and pray that you have the strength
    to escape the tribulations that are imminent
    and to stand before the Son of Man."

The Gospel of the Lord.

EXPLANATION OF THE READING

Jesus' words to his disciples serve as a warning about the coming of
the Son of Man. The reference to "the roaring of the sea and the waves"
and the subsequent examples that call for us to stay awake may seem
alarming, but they are not meant to frighten us. We are called to be
prepared at all times so that when the Lord comes, we are ready. What
advances or contributes to our readiness for the Lord's coming? Do we
enter this season with a sense of resolve and urgency to be prepared?
How can we keep a watchful eye for him this day?

December 8, 2018

IMMACULATE CONCEPTION OF THE BLESSED VIRGIN MARY

PATRONAL FEASTDAY OF THE UNITED STATES OF AMERICA

A reading from the holy Gospel according to Luke   1:26–38

The angel Gabriel was sent from God
    to a town of Galilee called Nazareth,
    to a virgin betrothed to a man named Joseph,
    of the house of David,
    and the virgin's name was Mary.
And coming to her, he said,
    "Hail, full of grace! The Lord is with you."

But she was greatly troubled at what was said
    and pondered what sort of greeting this might be.
Then the angel said to her,
    "Do not be afraid, Mary,
    for you have found favor with God.
Behold, you will conceive in your womb and bear a son,
    and you shall name him Jesus.
He will be great and will be called Son of the Most High,
    and the Lord God will give him the throne of David
        his father,
    and he will rule over the house of Jacob forever,
    and of his Kingdom there will be no end."
But Mary said to the angel,
    "How can this be,
    since I have no relations with a man?"
And the angel said to her in reply,
    "The Holy Spirit will come upon you,
    and the power of the Most High will overshadow you.
Therefore the child to be born
    will be called holy, the Son of God.
And behold, Elizabeth, your relative,
    has also conceived a son in her old age,
    and this is the sixth month for her who was called barren;
    for nothing will be impossible for God."
Mary said, "Behold, I am the handmaid of the Lord.
May it be done to me according to your word."
Then the angel departed from her.

The Gospel of the Lord.

EXPLANATION OF THE READING

The angel Gabriel greeted Mary with the words, "Hail, full of grace! The Lord is with you." What must it have been like for Mary to encounter an angel in her home in Nazareth? Is it possible to be happy and scared at the same time? Did Mary find solace in the words of Gabriel acknowledging that she was full of grace, blessed by God? The angel also told her that the Lord was with her. Some days we may feel scared, unsure of what the future holds for us. May we take comfort in knowing that the Lord is near to us, especially in times of fear and worry, as well as in times of great joy.

December 9, 2018

SECOND SUNDAY OF ADVENT

A reading from the holy Gospel according to Luke   3:1–6

In the fifteenth year of the reign of Tiberius Caesar,
    when Pontius Pilate was governor of Judea,
    and Herod was tetrarch of Galilee,
    and his brother Philip tetrarch of the region of
        Ituraea and Trachonitis,
    and Lysanias was tetrarch of Abilene,
    during the high priesthood of Annas and Caiaphas,
    the word of God came to John the son of Zechariah
        in the desert.
John went throughout the whole region of the Jordan,
    proclaiming a baptism of repentance for
        the forgiveness of sins,
    as it is written in the book of the words of
        the prophet Isaiah:

A voice of one crying out in the desert:
"Prepare the way of the Lord,
*   make straight his paths.*
Every valley shall be filled
*   and every mountain and hill shall be made low.*
The winding roads shall be made straight,
*   and the rough ways made smooth,*
and all flesh shall see the salvation of God."

The Gospel of the Lord.

EXPLANATION OF THE READING

John identifies himself as a prophet by quoting the prophet Isaiah, who, like John, began his prophetic ministry in a time when Israel is under the control of a foreign power. In John's time, the Roman emperor reigned, and a Roman governor ruled Judea; even the Jewish leaders were obedient to Rome. John calls the Jewish people to be ready when God comes to rule over his people by repentance and making what is crooked straight and what is rough smooth. He later speaks of the one who is to come after John, one already among them whom they do not recognize. In Advent, we too remember that we are to be ready when God comes to reign. We hear the stories again remember all that happened before Jesus' birth and after, and we prepare in faith and hope for when he will come again in glory. Those of us who suffer illness or weakness live in a constant waiting. May we be signs of patience and hope to those we welcome into our world and look for the ways Christ is present to us now.

December 16, 2018

THIRD SUNDAY OF ADVENT

A reading from the holy Gospel according to Luke   3:10–18

The crowds asked John the Baptist,
    "What should we do?"
He said to them in reply,
    "Whoever has two cloaks
    should share with the person who has none.
And whoever has food should do likewise."
Even tax collectors came to be baptized and they said to him,
    "Teacher, what should we do?"
He answered them,
    "Stop collecting more than what is prescribed."
Soldiers also asked him,
    "And what is it that we should do?"
He told them,
    "Do not practice extortion,
    do not falsely accuse anyone,
    and be satisfied with your wages."

Now the people were filled with expectation,
    and all were asking in their hearts
    whether John might be the Christ.
John answered them all, saying,
    "I am baptizing you with water,
    but one mightier than I is coming.
I am not worthy to loosen the thongs of his sandals.
He will baptize you with the Holy Spirit and fire.

His winnowing fan is in his hand to clear his threshing floor
and to gather the wheat into his barn,
but the chaff he will burn with unquenchable fire."
Exhorting them in many other ways,
he preached good news to the people.

The Gospel of the Lord.

EXPLANATION OF THE READING

"What should we do?" is the question presented to John the Baptist
this week. His reply is that—no matter what your role in life, be it a
tax collector, a soldier or a member of the crowd—we are to follow the
example of love. Our response is our acceptance of that great love or our
rejection of it. It is our choice whether we live in his love or live separated
from it.

Through Baptism, we become a member of the Shepherd's flock. As a
part of the sheepfold, we enter a relationship with the community and
we come to know how we are to live in that community.

December 23, 2018

FOURTH SUNDAY OF ADVENT

A reading from the holy Gospel according to Luke   1:39–45

Mary set out
and traveled to the hill country in haste
to a town of Judah,
where she entered the house of Zechariah
and greeted Elizabeth.

When Elizabeth heard Mary's greeting,
  the infant leaped in her womb,
  and Elizabeth, filled with the Holy Spirit,
  cried out in a loud voice and said,
  "Blessed are you among women,
  and blessed is the fruit of your womb.
And how does this happen to me,
  that the mother of my Lord should come to me?
For at the moment the sound of your greeting reached my ears,
  the infant in my womb leaped for joy.
Blessed are you who believed
  that what was spoken to you by the Lord
  would be fulfilled."

The Gospel of the Lord.

EXPLANATION OF THE READING

Elizabeth greets Mary, her much younger relative, with the words, "Blessed are you among women and blessed is the fruit of your womb." Her exuberant greeting is followed by a somewhat mystified question: "How does this happen to me, that the mother of my Lord should come to me?" How often do we have similar thoughts: Who am I? Am I worthy to be in the presence of my Lord? Jesus, in his love and his mercy, desires to be with us. As on that day when these two mothers met, and Jesus brought blessings to Zechariah and Elizabeth's home, Jesus brings blessings to us and our homes. When we gather as Christ's family at Mass and anytime two or three are gathered in his name, he is present, and he blesses us with his love and grace.

CHRISTMAS TIME

December 25, 2018

NATIVITY OF THE LORD

A reading from the holy Gospel according to Luke   Luke 2:1–14

In those days a decree went out from Caesar Augustus
    that the whole world should be enrolled.
This was the first enrollment,
    when Quirinius was governor of Syria.
So all went to be enrolled, each to his own town.
And Joseph too went up from Galilee from the town
      of Nazareth
    to Judea, to the city of David that is called Bethlehem,
    because he was of the house and family of David,
    to be enrolled with Mary, his betrothed, who was with child.
While they were there,
    the time came for her to have her child,
    and she gave birth to her firstborn son.
She wrapped him in swaddling clothes and laid him
      in a manger,
    because there was no room for them in the inn.

Now there were shepherds in that region living in the fields
    and keeping the night watch over their flock.
The angel of the Lord appeared to them
    and the glory of the Lord shone around them,
    and they were struck with great fear.

The angel said to them,
   "Do not be afraid;
   for behold, I proclaim to you good news of great joy
   that will be for all the people.
For today in the city of David
   a savior has been born for you who is Christ and Lord.
And this will be a sign for you:
   you will find an infant wrapped in swaddling clothes
   and lying in a manger."
And suddenly there was a multitude of
      the heavenly host with the angel,
   praising God and saying:
      "Glory to God in the highest
         and on earth peace to those on whom
            his favor rests."

The Gospel of the Lord.

This reading was taken from the Mass during the Night.

EXPLANATION OF THE READING

Today we hear the good news of the birth of Jesus. He is born in Bethlehem, which means "house of bread," how fitting for the One who would later be called the Bread of Life. The prophets foretold that the Messiah would be born in Bethlehem, the city of David, his ancestor. David was a shepherd boy who later became the greatest king of Israel. Jesus also identifies with David, referring to himself as the Good Shepherd. At his crucifixion, he is given the title King of the Jews, and later the Church proclaims him Christ the King. The prophets foretold that the Savior would be royalty and given the name "Prince of Peace." This small child born in Bethlehem is given many names, and he fulfills them all. May we rejoice today in the good news of the birth of Jesus, whom we call Savior and Lord, and who calls each of us by name.

HOLY FAMILY OF JESUS, MARY, AND JOSEPH

A reading from the holy Gospel according to Luke   2:41–52

Each year Jesus' parents went to Jerusalem for
      the feast of Passover,
   and when he was twelve years old,
   they went up according to festival custom.
After they had completed its days,
      as they were returning,
   the boy Jesus remained behind in Jerusalem,
   but his parents did not know it.
Thinking that he was in the caravan,
   they journeyed for a day
   and looked for him among their relatives and
      acquaintances,
   but not finding him,
   they returned to Jerusalem to look for him.
After three days they found him in the temple,
   sitting in the midst of the teachers,
   listening to them and asking them questions,
   and all who heard him were astounded
   at his understanding and his answers.
When his parents saw him,
   they were astonished,
   and his mother said to him,
   "Son, why have you done this to us?
Your father and I have been looking for you with
      great anxiety."

And he said to them,
   "Why were you looking for me?
Did you not know that I must be in
   my Father's house?"
But they did not understand what he said to them.
He went down with them and came to Nazareth,
   and was obedient to them;
   and his mother kept all these things in her heart.
And Jesus advanced in wisdom and age and favor
   before God and man.

The Gospel of the Lord.

EXPLANATION OF THE READING

As the holy family was returning from Jerusalem back to Nazareth, Mary and Joseph were not aware that the twelve-year-old Jesus had remained behind. Imagine the parents' panic as they searched for their son. Three days of searching led them back to Jerusalem, where they found the child in the temple as he sat amid the teachers. We may become anxious when we expect to find something in one place and it is not there anymore. We wonder where it could be. Did someone take it? Who did not return it to its rightful place? Even in our moments of forgetfulness, our God never forgets us. May you rest today in remembering that you are remembered and loved by the God of all time and memory.

January 1, 2019

MARY, THE HOLY MOTHER OF GOD

A reading from the holy Gospel according to Luke   2:16–21

The shepherds went in haste to Bethlehem and found
    Mary and Joseph,
  and the infant lying in the manger.
When they saw this,
  they made known the message
  that had been told them about this child.
All who heard it were amazed
  by what had been told them by the shepherds.
And Mary kept all these things,
  reflecting on them in her heart.
Then the shepherds returned,
  glorifying and praising God
  for all they had heard and seen,
  just as it had been told to them.

When eight days were completed for his circumcision,
  he was named Jesus, the name given him by the angel
  before he was conceived in the womb.

The Gospel of the Lord.

EXPLANATION OF THE READING

When the shepherds left Bethlehem, they "returned, glorifying and praising God for all they had heard and seen, just as it had been told to them." All that the shepherds had experienced that holy night— the angels, their journey to Bethlehem, their finding the Holy Family there—calls for a response. In what ways do we encounter the Divine? In the beauty of the liturgy, in the love of family and friends, in quiet moments of prayer? What is our response to an encounter with the

Divine? How often have we been so moved by that encounter that we offer God glory and praise? When we honor God in this way, we are speaking to him, but we are also speaking to others about him. May the coming week be filled with opportunity for you to share the joy of God with those you meet.

January 6, 2019

EPIPHANY OF THE LORD

A reading from the holy Gospel according to Matthew   2:1–12

When Jesus was born in Bethlehem of Judea,
    in the days of King Herod,
    behold, magi from the east arrived in Jerusalem, saying,
    "Where is the newborn king of the Jews?
We saw his star at its rising
    and have come to do him homage."
When King Herod heard this,
    he was greatly troubled,
    and all Jerusalem with him.
Assembling all the chief priests and the scribes
        of the people,
    he inquired of them where the Christ was to be born.
They said to him, "In Bethlehem of Judea,
    for thus it has been written through the prophet:
    And you, Bethlehem, land of Judah,
        are by no means least among the rulers of Judah;
    since from you shall come a ruler,
        who is to shepherd my people Israel."

Then Herod called the magi secretly
 and ascertained from them the time of
  the star's appearance.
He sent them to Bethlehem and said,
 "Go and search diligently for the child.
When you have found him, bring me word,
 that I too may go and do him homage."
After their audience with the king they set out.
And behold, the star that they had seen at its rising
  preceded them,
 until it came and stopped over the place where
  the child was.
They were overjoyed at seeing the star,
 and on entering the house
 they saw the child with Mary his mother.
They prostrated themselves and did him homage.
Then they opened their treasures
 and offered him gifts of gold, frankincense,
  and myrrh.
And having been warned in a dream not to return to Herod,
 they departed for their country by another way.

The Gospel of the Lord.

EXPLANATION OF THE READING

The Magi, visitors from the East, follow a star to Bethlehem, where they find the child with Mary, his mother. They prostrated themselves, which means to be face down, level with the ground, to show him honor and respect. They presented him with gifts of gold, frankincense, and myrrh. When we are in the presence of the Lord, how do we honor him? What gifts can we offer? The Magi attempted to make themselves small and low to the ground, in front of the one who was so great. Like the Magi, we search for Jesus, too. How do we respond when we find him? What could we offer to show that we recognize the true identity of this Child?

January 13, 2019

BAPTISM OF THE LORD

**A reading from the holy Gospel
according to Luke**   3:15–16, 21–22

The people were filled with expectation,
   and all were asking in their hearts
   whether John might be the Christ.
John answered them all, saying,
   "I am baptizing you with water,
   but one mightier than I is coming.
I am not worthy to loosen the thongs of his sandals.
He will baptize you with the Holy Spirit and fire."

After all the people had been baptized
   and Jesus also had been baptized and was praying,
   heaven was opened and the Holy Spirit descended upon him
   in bodily form like a dove.
And a voice came from heaven,
   "You are my beloved Son;
   with you I am well pleased."

The Gospel of the Lord.

EXPLANATION OF THE READING

Those gathered at the Jordan River wonder about John the Baptist's
identity. He responds that he baptizes with water, but the one who is to
come after him will baptize with fire and the spirit. The image of fire has
a prominent place in Scripture, revealing an encounter with God,
particularly the outpouring of the Holy Spirit at Pentecost. The abundant
outpouring of the Spirit is an indication of the continuing action of
Christ through us, his people, his Church. In our own Baptism in water,
we are united in a profound way with Jesus through the action of the
Spirit. May we continue to be transformed by the elements of creation
and the work of the Spirit.

Ordinary Time during Winter

January 20, 2019

Second Sunday in Ordinary Time

A reading from the holy Gospel according to John   2:1–11

There was a wedding at Cana in Galilee,
   and the mother of Jesus was there.
Jesus and his disciples were also invited to the wedding.
When the wine ran short,
   the mother of Jesus said to him,
   "They have no wine."
And Jesus said to her,
   "Woman, how does your concern affect me?
My hour has not yet come."
His mother said to the servers,
   "Do whatever he tells you."
Now there were six stone water jars there for
     Jewish ceremonial washings,
   each holding twenty to thirty gallons.
Jesus told them,
   "Fill the jars with water."
So they filled them to the brim.
Then he told them,
   "Draw some out now and take it to the headwaiter."

So they took it.
And when the headwaiter tasted the water that
      had become wine,
   without knowing where it came from
   —although the servers who had drawn the water knew—,
   the headwaiter called the bridegroom and said to him,
   "Everyone serves good wine first,
   and then when people have drunk freely, an inferior one;
   but you have kept the good wine until now."
Jesus did this as the beginning of his signs at Cana in Galilee
   and so revealed his glory,
   and his disciples began to believe in him.

The Gospel of the Lord.

EXPLANATION OF THE READING

Today's Gospel is set at a wedding feast, where Jesus is asked by his
mother to assist in what would become an uncomfortable and possibly
disgraceful situation: running out of wine. In response, Jesus miraculously
provides a vast amount of wine. This offers us a glimpse of the great
abundance of God's Kingdom. How can we respond to the needs of
those around us? When there is a lack or deficiency, our own response
may not seem adequate but we know that the Lord can transform our
efforts. How are we called, through our responses to the needs of others,
to build the Kingdom this week? How can we allow others to build the
Kingdom as we respond to our needs?

January 27, 2019

Third Sunday in Ordinary Time

A reading from the holy Gospel according to Luke 1:1–4; 4:14–21

Since many have undertaken to compile
    a narrative of the events
that have been fulfilled among us,
just as those who were eyewitnesses from the beginning
and ministers of the word have handed them down to us,
I too have decided,
after investigating everything accurately anew,
to write it down in an orderly sequence for you,
most excellent Theophilus,
so that you may realize the certainty of the teachings
you have received.

Jesus returned to Galilee in the power of the Spirit,
    and news of him spread throughout the whole region.
He taught in their synagogues and was praised by all.

He came to Nazareth, where he had grown up,
    and went according to his custom
into the synagogue on the sabbath day.
He stood up to read and was handed a scroll of
    the prophet Isaiah.
He unrolled the scroll and found the passage where it
    was written:
    The Spirit of the Lord is upon me,
      because he has anointed me
      to bring glad tidings to the poor.

> He has sent me to proclaim liberty to captives
>   and recovery of sight to the blind,
>   to let the oppressed go free,
>   and to proclaim a year acceptable to the Lord.
Rolling up the scroll, he handed it back to the
    attendant and sat down,
  and the eyes of all in the synagogue looked intently at him.
He said to them,
    "Today this Scripture passage is fulfilled in
       your hearing."

The Gospel of the Lord.

EXPLANATION OF THE READING

Jesus enters the synagogue in Nazareth on the Sabbath, as he was in the habit of doing. He unrolled the scroll and read from the prophet Isaiah, who writes of his anointing to bring glad tidings to the poor, liberty to captives, healing to the sick, and freedom to the oppressed, as well as of his proclaiming a year acceptable to the Lord. Jesus is announcing that his own mission will be a continuation of what began with Isaiah. This tradition of proclaiming the Word of God has now been handed on to us; and today we, as individuals and as a community, continue to discover in Sacred Scripture God's charge for our lives. As we accept Jesus mission as our own, how can we bring gladness, hope, and healing to another, even in our own weakness?

February 3, 2019

Fourth Sunday in Ordinary Time

A reading from the holy Gospel according to Luke   4:21–30

Jesus began speaking in the synagogue, saying:
  "Today this Scripture passage is fulfilled in your hearing."
And all spoke highly of him
  and were amazed at the gracious words that
    came from his mouth.
They also asked, "Isn't this the son of Joseph?"
He said to them, "Surely you will quote me this proverb,
  'Physician, cure yourself,' and say,
  'Do here in your native place
  the things that we heard were done in Capernaum.'"
And he said, "Amen, I say to you,
  no prophet is accepted in his own native place.
Indeed, I tell you,
  there were many widows in Israel in the days of Elijah
  when the sky was closed for three and a half years
  and a severe famine spread over the entire land.
It was to none of these that Elijah was sent,
  but only to a widow in Zarephath in the land of Sidon.
Again, there were many lepers in Israel
  during the time of Elisha the prophet;
  yet not one of them was cleansed, but only
    Naaman the Syrian."
When the people in the synagogue heard this,
  they were all filled with fury.

They rose up, drove him out of the town,
   and led him to the brow of the hill
   on which their town had been built,
   to hurl him down headlong.
But Jesus passed through the midst of them and
      went away.

The Gospel of the Lord.

EXPLANATION OF THE READING

At first, the people of Nazareth respond favorably to Jesus' words, but before long they are furious with him and want to fling him down a hill at the edge of town. What could possibly have caused such a reaction? He disappointed them by not doing for them the kinds of miracles he had done elsewhere. And he challenged them by pointing out that Scripture shows that God's care is not just for them, but for all people, Jewish or not. Do we ever find ourselves responding like the townspeople of Nazareth? Sometimes the words of Jesus are difficult for us to hear and we would rather not follow where he is leading us. Let us try this week to trust his words and to follow his voice. How can we allow his word to influence and transform us?

February 10, 2019

FIFTH SUNDAY IN ORDINARY TIME

A reading from the holy Gospel according to Luke   5:1–11

While the crowd was pressing in on Jesus and listening to
      the word of God,
   he was standing by the Lake of Gennesaret.
He saw two boats there alongside the lake;
   the fishermen had disembarked and were washing
      their nets.

Getting into one of the boats, the one belonging to Simon,
  he asked him to put out a short distance from the shore.
Then he sat down and taught the crowds from the boat.
After he had finished speaking, he said to Simon,
  "Put out into deep water and lower your nets for a catch."
Simon said in reply,
  "Master, we have worked hard all night and have
    caught nothing,
  but at your command I will lower the nets."
When they had done this, they caught a great number of fish
  and their nets were tearing.
They signaled to their partners in the other boat
  to come to help them.
They came and filled both boats
  so that the boats were in danger of sinking.
When Simon Peter saw this, he fell at the knees
    of Jesus and said,
  "Depart from me, Lord, for I am a sinful man."
For astonishment at the catch of fish they had made
    seized him
  and all those with him,
  and likewise James and John, the sons of Zebedee,
  who were partners of Simon.
Jesus said to Simon, "Do not be afraid;
  from now on you will be catching men."
When they brought their boats to the shore,
  they left everything and followed him.

The Gospel of the Lord.

EXPLANATION OF THE READING

While preaching to a large crowd near the lakeshore, Jesus's notices two empty boats and some fishermen washing their nets. Jesus steps into one of the boats and asks Simon, the boat's owner, to sail out into the lake a bit so he can address the crowd more easily. When he is done preaching, Jesus asks them to sail a bit deeper and lower their nets yet again. They had been fishing all night and caught nothing, but Peter grudgingly obeys and caught so many fish that it nearly sank Simon's boat and a second one. When they arrived on shore, all the fishermen left everything behind to follow Jesus to "catch" people and lead them to Jesus. When Jesus steps into our lives, he calls us to himself and calls us to lead others to him. He shows us that he will give us all we need, even when we think we have nothing. Consider how you can invite people to follow Jesus.

February 17, 2019

SIXTH SUNDAY IN ORDINARY TIME

A reading from the holy Gospel according to Luke   6:17, 20–26

Jesus came down with the Twelve
    and stood on a stretch of level ground
    with a great crowd of his disciples
    and a large number of the people
    from all Judea and Jerusalem
    and the coastal region of Tyre and Sidon.
And raising his eyes toward his disciples he said:
        "Blessed are you who are poor,
            for the kingdom of God is yours.
        Blessed are you who are now hungry,
            for you will be satisfied.
        Blessed are you who are now weeping,
            for you will laugh.

Blessed are you when people hate you,
     and when they exclude and insult you,
     and denounce your name as evil
     on account of the Son of Man.
Rejoice and leap for joy on that day!
Behold, your reward will be great in heaven.
For their ancestors treated the prophets in the same way.
     But woe to you who are rich,
          for you have received your consolation.
     Woe to you who are filled now,
          for you will be hungry.
     Woe to you who laugh now,
          for you will grieve and weep.
     Woe to you when all speak well of you,
          for their ancestors treated the false prophets in this way."

The Gospel of the Lord.

EXPLANATION OF THE READING

In today's Gospel, Jesus presents us with four blessings, or beatitudes, and four woes. Times of blessings bring us happiness and joy; woes offers us distress and sorrow. In our day-to-day living, we experience both blessings and woes, but our list would probably not match Jesus' list. It seems odd to hear that it is a blessing to be poor, hungry, weeping, and hated by others, while having a full stomach, and being content and satisfied are dangerous for us. When we are content and self-satisfied, we may tend to forget about our need for God. Our hardships are not God's doing, but they do remind us that we are always in need of him. May our prayers be full of gratitude for what God has given us, and may we trust that he will always be with us in difficult times.

February 24, 2019

SEVENTH SUNDAY IN ORDINARY TIME

A reading from the holy Gospel according to Luke   6:27–38

Jesus said to his disciples:
   "To you who hear I say,
      love your enemies, do good to those who hate you,
      bless those who curse you, pray for those who mistreat you.
To the person who strikes you on one cheek,
      offer the other one as well,
      and from the person who takes your cloak,
      do not withhold even your tunic.
Give to everyone who asks of you,
      and from the one who takes what is yours
         do not demand it back.
Do to others as you would have them do to you.
For if you love those who love you,
      what credit is that to you?
Even sinners love those who love them.
And if you do good to those who do good to you,
      what credit is that to you?
Even sinners do the same.
If you lend money to those from whom you
         expect repayment,
      what credit is that to you?
Even sinners lend to sinners,
      and get back the same amount.

But rather, love your enemies and do good to them,
    and lend expecting nothing back;
    then your reward will be great
    and you will be children of the Most High,
    for he himself is kind to the ungrateful and the wicked.
Be merciful, just as your Father is merciful.

"Stop judging and you will not be judged.
Stop condemning and you will not be condemned.
Forgive and you will be forgiven.
Give and gifts will be given to you;
    a good measure, packed together, shaken down,
        and overflowing,
    will be poured into your lap.
For the measure with which you measure
    will in return be measured out to you."

The Gospel of the Lord.

EXPLANATION OF THE READING

Today's reading from Luke's account of the Gospel epitomizes what it means to be a follower of Jesus Christ—love your enemies, turn the other cheek, give to those who ask, do as you would have them do unto you, lend without expecting repayment, judge not lest you be judged. With these words, we are called to love others as God loves. Those can be difficult expectations for us, especially when we are weak or unwell, but we are called to put them into practice. These verses help us find our place in creation and work toward harmony and the fulfillment of God's plan. May our thoughts actions this week contribute to the order, peace, and harmony of the world, as well as to our own peacefulness as we live as his disciples.

March 3, 2019

Eighth Sunday in Ordinary Time

A reading from the holy Gospel according to Luke 6:39–45

Jesus told his disciples a parable,
   "Can a blind person guide a blind person?
Will not both fall into a pit?
No disciple is superior to the teacher;
   but when fully trained,
   every disciple will be like his teacher.
Why do you notice the splinter in your brother's eye,
   but do not perceive the wooden beam in your own?
How can you say to your brother,
   'Brother, let me remove that splinter in your eye,'
   when you do not even notice the wooden beam in your
      own eye?
You hypocrite! Remove the wooden beam from your eye first;
   then you will see clearly
   to remove the splinter in your brother's eye.
A good tree does not bear rotten fruit,
   nor does a rotten tree bear good fruit.
For every tree is known by its own fruit.
For people do not pick figs from thornbushes,
   nor do they gather grapes from brambles.
A good person out of the store of goodness in his heart
      produces good,
   but an evil person out of a store of evil produces evil;
   for from the fullness of the heart the mouth speaks."

The Gospel of the Lord.

EXPLANATION OF THE READING

Splinters, planks, brambles, trees that bear good fruit and bad—we can see how Jesus' early life as a carpenter's son influenced the imagery he uses in his preaching. Like a tree that is known by its fruit, a person's heart will reveal itself in good actions or evil. We must take time to look at the fruit of our lives. If it is good, we continue to live as we have been and strive to grow in virtue. If the fruit is bad—discord or dishonesty, for example—we must change our hearts. We are never static, we are either growing or diminishing. Even in our times of sickness or weakness, we can strengthen our souls with gratitude for the all the goodness God has shown us through our lives and repentance for the times when we have not shown that goodness to others. God feeds us and prunes us so that we may bear life-giving fruit to share with others, whatever our circumstances.

LENT

March 10, 2019

FIRST SUNDAY OF LENT

A reading from the holy Gospel according to Luke   4:1–13

Filled with the Holy Spirit, Jesus returned from the Jordan
    and was led by the Spirit into the desert for forty days,
    to be tempted by the devil.
He ate nothing during those days,
    and when they were over he was hungry.
The devil said to him,
    "If you are the Son of God,
    command this stone to become bread."
Jesus answered him,
    "It is written, *One does not live on bread alone.*"
Then he took him up and showed him
    all the kingdoms of the world in a single instant.
The devil said to him,
    "I shall give to you all this power and glory;
    for it has been handed over to me,
    and I may give it to whomever I wish.
All this will be yours, if you worship me."
Jesus said to him in reply,
    "It is written:
        You shall worship the Lord, your God,
        and him alone shall you serve."

Then he led him to Jerusalem,
    made him stand on the parapet of the temple,
        and said to him,
"If you are the Son of God,
throw yourself down from here, for it is written:
    He will command his angels concerning you,
        to guard you,
and:
    With their hands they will support you,
    lest you dash your foot against a stone."
Jesus said to him in reply,
    "It also says,
    You shall not put the Lord, your God, to the test."
When the devil had finished every temptation,
    he departed from him for a time.

The Gospel of the Lord.

EXPLANATION OF THE READING

After Jesus was baptized by John in the Jordan River, the Holy Spirit led him into the desert to be tempted. The strength and fidelity that Jesus showed when the devil tempted came at the end of his period of solitude. Sometimes God calls us to a place where we may feel alone and isolated. Like Jesus' time in the desert, we know that we are not truly alone. In this solitary time, we may more easily focus our hearts and minds on the Lord. The seclusion that we may experience is an opportunity to be faithful in our relationship with God, to remember that he is very near to us and he will take care of us.

March 17, 2019

Second Sunday of Lent

A reading from the holy Gospel according to Luke   9:28b–36

Jesus took Peter, John, and James
    and went up the mountain to pray.
While he was praying, his face changed in appearance
    and his clothing became dazzling white.
And behold, two men were conversing with him,
      Moses and Elijah,
    who appeared in glory and spoke of his exodus
    that he was going to accomplish in Jerusalem.
Peter and his companions had been overcome
      by sleep,
    but becoming fully awake,
    they saw his glory and the two men standing with him.
As they were about to part from him,
      Peter said to Jesus,
    "Master, it is good that we are here;
    let us make three tents,
    one for you, one for Moses, and one for Elijah."
But he did not know what he was saying.
While he was still speaking,
    a cloud came and cast a shadow over them,
    and they became frightened when they entered the cloud.
Then from the cloud came a voice that said,
    "This is my chosen Son; listen to him."
After the voice had spoken, Jesus was found alone.
They fell silent and did not at that time
    tell anyone what they had seen.

The Gospel of the Lord.

EXPLANATION OF THE READING

It seems that whenever we fight to stay awake, the more difficult it becomes for us to keep our eyes open. In today's Gospel, we hear how "Peter and his companions were overcome by sleep," though they did manage wake in time to experience the Transfiguration. As disciples, we are all called to follow the Lord, but there are moments on that journey that cause weariness. Let us keep our eyes open to see how God is revealed to us this week. May we have the eyes of faith to see the radiant alongside the ordinary. And may he allow us to find comfort and rest in the Glorified Christ.

March 24, 2019

THIRD SUNDAY OF LENT

A reading from the holy Gospel according to Luke   13:1–9

Some people told Jesus about the Galileans
   whose blood Pilate had mingled with the blood of
     their sacrifices.
Jesus said to them in reply,
   "Do you think that because these Galileans
     suffered in this way
   they were greater sinners than all other Galileans?
By no means!
But I tell you, if you do not repent,
   you will all perish as they did!
Or those eighteen people who were killed
   when the tower at Siloam fell on them—
   do you think they were more guilty
   than everyone else who lived in Jerusalem?
By no means!

But I tell you, if you do not repent,
   you will all perish as they did!"

And he told them this parable:
   "There once was a person who had a fig tree planted in his
      orchard,
   and when he came in search of fruit on it but
      found none,
   he said to the gardener,
   'For three years now I have come in search of fruit on this
      fig tree
   but have found none.
So cut it down.
Why should it exhaust the soil?'
He said to him in reply,
   'Sir, leave it for this year also,
   and I shall cultivate the ground around it and fertilize it;
   it may bear fruit in the future.
If not you can cut it down.'"

The Gospel of the Lord.

EXPLANATION OF THE READING

What are the conditions that determine whether a fig tree would produce fruit? We know that a tree must reach a certain age before it can produce figs; too much nitrogen in the soil will allow the tree to be green and lush but not bear fruit; and too much or too little water will stop the tree from producing fruit. Though the parable of the fig tree is about more than just gardening, the details may help. Are there moments when we are not bearing fruit? What are we lacking, or what do we have too much of? The Master Gardener will, if we let him, nourish us, give us what we need, and take away what hinders us so that we might yield figs. We are grateful that the Lord offers us a second and even third chance when we fail. Let us pray this week for God to help us and to be patient with us.

March 31, 2019

Fourth Sunday of Lent

A reading from the holy Gospel according to Luke 15:1–3, 11–32

Tax collectors and sinners were all drawing near to
    listen to Jesus,
  but the Pharisees and scribes began to complain, saying,
  "This man welcomes sinners and eats with them."
So to them Jesus addressed this parable:
"A man had two sons, and the younger son said to his father,
  'Father give me the share of your estate that should
    come to me.'
So the father divided the property between them.
After a few days, the younger son collected all his belongings
    and set off to a distant country
  where he squandered his inheritance on a life
    of dissipation.
When he had freely spent everything,
  a severe famine struck that country,
  and he found himself in dire need.
So he hired himself out to one of the local citizens
  who sent him to his farm to tend the swine.
And he longed to eat his fill of the pods on which
    the swine fed,
  but nobody gave him any.
Coming to his senses he thought,
  'How many of my father's hired workers
  have more than enough food to eat,
  but here am I, dying from hunger.
I shall get up and go to my father and I shall say to him,
  "Father, I have sinned against heaven and against you.

I no longer deserve to be called your son;
    treat me as you would treat one of your hired workers.'"
So he got up and went back to his father.
While he was still a long way off,
    his father caught sight of him, and was filled
        with compassion.
He ran to his son, embraced him and kissed him.
His son said to him,
    'Father, I have sinned against heaven and against you;
    I no longer deserve to be called your son.'
But his father ordered his servants,
    'Quickly bring the finest robe and put it on him;
    put a ring on his finger and sandals on his feet.
Take the fattened calf and slaughter it.
Then let us celebrate with a feast,
    because this son of mine was dead, and has come to
        life again;
    he was lost, and has been found.'
Then the celebration began.
Now the older son had been out in the field
    and, on his way back, as he neared the house,
    he heard the sound of music and dancing.
He called one of the servants and asked what this might mean.
The servant said to him,
    'Your brother has returned
    and your father has slaughtered the fattened calf
    because he has him back safe and sound.'
He became angry,
    and when he refused to enter the house,
    his father came out and pleaded with him.

He said to his father in reply,
    'Look, all these years I served you
    and not once did I disobey your orders;
    yet you never gave me even a young goat to
        feast on with my friends.
But when your son returns
    who swallowed up your property with prostitutes,
    for him you slaughter the fattened calf.'
He said to him,
    'My son, you are here with me always;
    everything I have is yours.
But now we must celebrate and rejoice,
    because your brother was dead and has come to life again;
    he was lost and has been found.'"

The Gospel of the Lord.

EXPLANATION OF THE READING

In the parable of the forgiving father, we are introduced to a family that experiences loss, forgiveness, and healing. We can imagine ourselves in the position of one or more of the characters in this story: a reckless son who acts rashly and later regrets his actions; the older son, who is dutiful to his father but becomes critical and resentful of the father's delight in his younger brother's homecoming; or the father, who faithfully and patiently awaits his son's return. Whichever character we can relate to, we have experienced the abundant love of God. Whether one is living as expected or on the periphery of society, God is generous with his love, and calls us to be equally generous. Let us pray this week for someone who has hurt us or someone we have hurt. When we do this, we will be imitating our merciful and compassionate God.

April 7, 2019

Fifth Sunday of Lent

A reading from the holy Gospel according to John   8:1–11

Jesus went to the Mount of Olives.
But early in the morning he arrived again in the temple area,
   and all the people started coming to him,
   and he sat down and taught them.
Then the scribes and the Pharisees brought a woman
   who had been caught in adultery
   and made her stand in the middle.
They said to him,
   "Teacher, this woman was caught
   in the very act of committing adultery.
Now in the law, Moses commanded us to stone such women.
So what do you say?"
They said this to test him,
   so that they could have some charge to bring against him.
Jesus bent down and began to write on the
     ground with his finger.
But when they continued asking him,
   he straightened up and said to them,
   "Let the one among you who is without sin
   be the first to throw a stone at her."
Again he bent down and wrote on the ground.
And in response, they went away one by one,
   beginning with the elders.
So he was left alone with the woman before him.
Then Jesus straightened up and said to her,
   "Woman, where are they?
Has no one condemned you?"

She replied, "No one, sir."
Then Jesus said, "Neither do I condemn you.
Go, and from now on do not sin any more."

The Gospel of the Lord.

EXPLANATION OF THE READING

Jesus is teaching at the temple in Jerusalem when group of scribes and Pharisees—powerful men—bring a woman to him, saying she had been caught in adultery. These men want Jesus to pass judgment on her. Jesus does not address the woman or the crowd, but simply bends down and begins to write on the ground with his finger. As the scribes and Pharisees continue to question him, he responds, "Let the one among you who is without sin be the first to throw a stone at her," and then bends down to write some more. One by one, the leaders leave; the elders go first because they, most of all, know how they have failed. We too must take the time to examine our lives and judge ourselves, not others, by the words of Jesus. If we fall short, we can rely on his forgiveness and compassion.

April 14, 2019

PALM SUNDAY

The Passion of our Lord Jesus Christ according to Luke   23:1–49

The elders of the people, chief priests and scribes,
    arose and brought Jesus before Pilate.
They brought charges against him, saying,
    "We found this man misleading our people;
    he opposes the payment of taxes to Caesar
    and maintains that he is the Christ, a king."

Pilate asked him, "Are you the king of the Jews?"
He said to him in reply, "You say so."
Pilate then addressed the chief priests and the crowds,
    "I find this man not guilty."
But they were adamant and said,
    "He is inciting the people with his teaching
        throughout all Judea,
    from Galilee where he began even to here."

On hearing this Pilate asked if the man was a Galilean;
    and upon learning that he was under Herod's jurisdiction,
    he sent him to Herod who was in Jerusalem at that time.
Herod was very glad to see Jesus;
    he had been wanting to see him for a long time,
    for he had heard about him
    and had been hoping to see him perform some sign.
He questioned him at length,
    but he gave him no answer.
The chief priests and scribes, meanwhile,
    stood by accusing him harshly.
Herod and his soldiers treated him contemptuously
        and mocked him,
    and after clothing him in resplendent garb,
    he sent him back to Pilate.
Herod and Pilate became friends that very day,
    even though they had been enemies formerly.
Pilate then summoned the chief priests, the rulers,
        and the people
    and said to them, "You brought this man to me
    and accused him of inciting the people to revolt.

I have conducted my investigation in your presence
    and have not found this man guilty
    of the charges you have brought against him,
    nor did Herod, for he sent him back to us.
So no capital crime has been committed by him.
Therefore I shall have him flogged and then release him."

But all together they shouted out,
    "Away with this man!
    Release Barabbas to us."
—Now Barabbas had been imprisoned for a rebellion
    that had taken place in the city and for murder.—
Again Pilate addressed them, still wishing to release Jesus,
    but they continued their shouting,
    "Crucify him! Crucify him!"
Pilate addressed them a third time,
    "What evil has this man done?
    I found him guilty of no capital crime.
Therefore I shall have him flogged and then release him."
With loud shouts, however,
    they persisted in calling for his crucifixion,
    and their voices prevailed.
The verdict of Pilate was that their demand should
        be granted.
So he released the man who had been imprisoned
    for rebellion and murder, for whom they asked,
    and he handed Jesus over to them to deal with
        as they wished.

As they led him away
　　they took hold of a certain Simon, a Cyrenian,
　　who was coming in from the country;
　　and after laying the cross on him,
　　they made him carry it behind Jesus.
A large crowd of people followed Jesus,
　　including many women who mourned and lamented him.
Jesus turned to them and said,
　　"Daughters of Jerusalem, do not weep for me;
　　weep instead for yourselves and for your children
　　for indeed, the days are coming when people
　　　will say,
　　'Blessed are the barren,
　　the wombs that never bore
　　and the breasts that never nursed.'
At that time people will say to the mountains,
　　'Fall upon us!'
　　and to the hills, 'Cover us!'
　　for if these things are done when the wood is green
　　what will happen when it is dry?"
Now two others, both criminals,
　　were led away with him to be executed.

When they came to the place called the Skull,
　　they crucified him and the criminals there,
　　one on his right, the other on his left.
Then Jesus said,
　　"Father, forgive them, they know not what they do."
They divided his garments by casting lots.

The people stood by and watched;
    the rulers, meanwhile, sneered at him and said,
    "He saved others, let him save himself
    if he is the chosen one, the Christ of God."
Even the soldiers jeered at him.
As they approached to offer him wine they called out,
    "If you are King of the Jews, save yourself."
Above him there was an inscription that read,
    "This is the King of the Jews."

Now one of the criminals hanging there reviled Jesus, saying,
    "Are you not the Christ?
    Save yourself and us."
The other, however, rebuking him, said in reply,
    "Have you no fear of God,
    for you are subject to the same condemnation?
And indeed, we have been condemned justly,
    for the sentence we received corresponds to our crimes,
    but this man has done nothing criminal."
Then he said,
    "Jesus, remember me when you come into your kingdom."
He replied to him,
    "Amen, I say to you,
    today you will be with me in Paradise."

It was now about noon and darkness came over
        the whole land
    until three in the afternoon
    because of an eclipse of the sun.
Then the veil of the temple was torn down the middle.

Jesus cried out in a loud voice,
"Father, into your hands I commend my spirit";
and when he had said this he breathed his last.

Here all kneel and pause for a short time.

The centurion who witnessed what had happened glorified
God and said,
"This man was innocent beyond doubt."
When all the people who had gathered for this spectacle saw
what had happened,
they returned home beating their breasts;
but all his acquaintances stood at a distance,
including the women who had followed him from Galilee
and saw these events.

The Gospel of the Lord.

Long form: Luke 22:14—23:56

EXPLANATION OF THE READING

The crowd that greets Jesus with cries of praise and songs of joy will,
by the end of the week, turn their shouts to accusations and allegations.
Our Lord and Savior knows what it is like to be praised one day and
faced with an angry mob another day. Yet, even in his suffering he offers
compassion and forgiveness. What is our response when we are faced
with frustration and anger? When we experience days of distress and
pain, are we able to look to our Lord's passion as a pattern of how to
respond? May this week offer you an opportunity to journey with the
Lord, offering forgiveness and peace to those amid their suffering and
your own.

EASTER TIME

April 21, 2019

EASTER SUNDAY OF THE RESURRECTION OF THE LORD

A reading from the holy Gospel according to John   20:1–9

On the first day of the week,
   Mary of Magdala came to the tomb early in the morning,
   while it was still dark,
   and saw the stone removed from the tomb.
So she ran and went to Simon Peter
   and to the other disciple whom Jesus loved, and told them,
   "They have taken the Lord from the tomb,
   and we don't know where they put him."
So Peter and the other disciple went out and came
      to the tomb.
They both ran, but the other disciple ran faster than Peter
   and arrived at the tomb first;
   he bent down and saw the burial cloths there,
      but did not go in.
When Simon Peter arrived after him,
   he went into the tomb and saw the burial cloths there,
   and the cloth that had covered his head,
   not with the burial cloths but rolled up in a separate place.
Then the other disciple also went in,
   the one who had arrived at the tomb first,
   and he saw and believed.

For they did not yet understand the Scripture
   that he had to rise from the dead.

The Gospel of the Lord.

This reading was taken from the morning Mass for Easter Day.

EXPLANATION OF THE READING

In the darkness of the early morning, Mary of Magdala went to the tomb. How shocking for her to see the stone removed from the entrance! She turns to Simon Peter and John for assistance. Like Mary of Magdala, when we encounter something that is alarming, perhaps even life-changing, we often turn to another for support and wisdom to help us discern what this means for us. On whom can we rely? God's Word, the sacraments, and fellow believers, individually and in the community of believers, the Church, offer this same support and wisdom when we encounter the presence of the Risen Christ through the joys, pains, sorrows, and surprises that come in every stage of our life.

April 28, 2019

SECOND SUNDAY OF EASTER

A reading from the holy Gospel according to John   20:19–31

On the evening of that first day of the week,
   when the doors were locked, where the disciples were,
   for fear of the Jews,
   Jesus came and stood in their midst
   and said to them, "Peace be with you."
When he had said this, he showed them his hands and his side.
The disciples rejoiced when they saw the Lord.
Jesus said to them again, "Peace be with you.
As the Father has sent me, so I send you."

And when he had said this, he breathed on
    them and said to them,
    "Receive the Holy Spirit.
Whose sins you forgive are forgiven them,
    and whose sins you retain are retained."

Thomas, called Didymus, one of the Twelve,
    was not with them when Jesus came.
So the other disciples said to him, "We have seen the Lord."
But he said to them,
    "Unless I see the mark of the nails in his hands
    and put my finger into the nailmarks
    and put my hand into his side, I will not believe."

Now a week later his disciples were again inside
    and Thomas was with them.
Jesus came, although the doors were locked,
    and stood in their midst and said, "Peace be with you."
Then he said to Thomas, "Put your finger here
        and see my hands,
    and bring your hand and put it into my side,
    and do not be unbelieving, but believe."
Thomas answered and said to him, "My Lord and my God!"
Jesus said to him, "Have you come to believe because you
        have seen me?
Blessed are those who have not seen and have believed."

Now Jesus did many other signs in the presence of his disciples
    that are not written in this book.
But these are written that you may come to believe
    that Jesus is the Christ, the Son of God,
    and that through this belief you may have life in his name.
The Gospel of the Lord.

EXPLANATION OF THE READING

Do you ever wonder how the other disciples responded to Thomas after his encounter with the Risen Lord? Did they look down upon him for not believing without seeing? Did they refrain from telling him, "We told you so!"? Whatever they thought, they remained in community with Thomas. They understood that it is only human to be filled with doubt and questions. It must have been especially so during the days right after the Jesus' death. Even we who profess the Resurrection of Jesus Christ will have times when doubt and uncertainty cloud our hearts and minds. Like Thomas, we may need to touch the Lord, perhaps in his presence in his word or in his people. With them, we say, "My Lord and my God," and accept the peace only he can bring.

May 5, 2019

THIRD SUNDAY OF EASTER

A reading from the holy Gospel according to John   21:1–14

At that time, Jesus revealed himself to his disciples at the
     Sea of Tiberias.
He revealed himself in this way.
Together were Simon Peter, Thomas called Didymus,
     Nathanael from Cana in Galilee,
     Zebedee's sons, and two others of his disciples.
Simon Peter said to them, "I am going fishing."
They said to him, "We also will come with you."
So they went out and got into the boat,
     but that night they caught nothing.
When it was already dawn, Jesus was standing on the shore;
     but the disciples did not realize that it was Jesus.
Jesus said to them, "Children, have you caught
     anything to eat?"
They answered him, "No."

So he said to them, "Cast the net over the right side of the boat
    and you will find something."
So they cast it, and were not able to pull it in
    because of the number of fish.
So the disciple whom Jesus loved said to Peter, "It is the Lord."
When Simon Peter heard that it was the Lord,
    he tucked in his garment, for he was lightly clad,
    and jumped into the sea.
The other disciples came in the boat,
    for they were not far from shore, only about a hundred yards,
    dragging the net with the fish.
When they climbed out on shore,
    they saw a charcoal fire with fish on it and bread.
Jesus said to them, "Bring some of the fish you just caught."
So Simon Peter went over and dragged the net ashore
    full of one hundred fifty-three large fish.
Even though there were so many, the net was not torn.
Jesus said to them, "Come, have breakfast."
And none of the disciples dared to ask him, "Who are you?"
    because they realized it was the Lord.
Jesus came over and took the bread and gave it to them,
    and in like manner the fish.
This was now the third time Jesus was revealed to
        his disciples
    after being raised from the dead.

The Gospel of the Lord.

Long form: John 21:1–19

EXPLANATION OF THE READING

After the Lord's Resurrection, Peter returns, at least temporarily, to his former profession as a fisherman. Even though he has already encountered the Risen Lord, Peter reverts to something familiar and trusted. After a long night of catching nothing, Peter follows Jesus' instruction to cast the net one more time. This time they caught so many fish that Peter could not pull the net into the boat. On hearing that it was the Lord, Peter's devotion to Jesus prompts him to jump in the water and pull the fish ashore. Peter's mission, whether catching fish or his new job of tending Jesus' flock, requires him to listen to the Lord's instructions. Let us pay close attention this week to the instructions the Lord may have for us and recognize his coming in the familiar moments of our day.

May 12, 2019

FOURTH SUNDAY OF EASTER

A reading from the holy Gospel according to John   10:27–30

Jesus said:
"My sheep hear my voice;
    I know them, and they follow me.
I give them eternal life, and they shall never perish.
No one can take them out of my hand.
My Father, who has given them to me, is greater than all,
    and no one can take them out of the Father's hand.
The Father and I are one."

The Gospel of the Lord.

EXPLANATION OF THE READING

The sheep hear the voice of the Good Shepherd and follow him. Sometimes it is difficult to hear the Shepherd's voice, especially when there are competing voices wanting our attention. How are we able to differentiate among all the voices we hear in our culture, our community, from caring neighbors, our friends, even family members? Whom do we follow? As his faithful sheep, how can we hear the voice of the Shepherd? Each time we open the Scriptures we are hearing the voice of the Shepherd. There is an intimacy between the Shepherd and the sheep. We follow him, he knows us by name. We can never be taken out of his hand. In our times of weakness, let us take comfort in the care of our Shepherd and his Father. And let us always keep in prayer all the members of his flock.

May 19, 2019

FIFTH SUNDAY OF EASTER

A reading from the holy Gospel according to John 13:31–33a, 34–35

When Judas had left them, Jesus said,
    "Now is the Son of Man glorified, and God
        is glorified in him.
If God is glorified in him,
    God will also glorify him in himself,
    and God will glorify him at once.
My children, I will be with you only a little while longer.
I give you a new commandment: love one another.
As I have loved you, so you also should love one another.
This is how all will know that you are my disciples,
    if you have love for one another."

The Gospel of the Lord.

EXPLANATION OF THE READING

Today's Gospel returns to the Last Supper, after Judas has left the scene. Jesus then gives a new commandment: to love one another as he has loved us. What can this mean, to love as Jesus has loved? During this meal, Jesus offers his followers his Body and his Blood—all of himself, everything he is. Not only does he offer us everything he is, he commands

us to love each other just as completely and selflessly as he does. This is
how we will be known as missionary disciples, by how we love one
another. May all those who are abandoned, rejected, or forsaken come
to know the love of Christ through his disciples.

May 26, 2019

SIXTH SUNDAY OF EASTER

A reading from the holy Gospel according to John 14:23–29

Jesus said to his disciples:
    "Whoever loves me will keep my word,
    and my Father will love him,
    and we will come to him and make our dwelling with him.
Whoever does not love me does not keep my words;
    yet the word you hear is not mine
    but that of the Father who sent me.

"I have told you this while I am with you.
The Advocate, the Holy Spirit,
    whom the Father will send in my name,
    will teach you everything
    and remind you of all that I told you.
Peace I leave with you; my peace I give to you.
Not as the world gives do I give it to you.
Do not let your hearts be troubled or afraid.
You heard me tell you,
    'I am going away and I will come back to you.'

If you loved me,
    you would rejoice that I am going to the Father;
    for the Father is greater than I.
And now I have told you this before it happens,
    so that when it happens you may believe."

The Gospel of the Lord.

EXPLANATION OF THE READING

Jesus makes a promise to his disciples, not only those gathered with him in that moment, but to us, too. He promises the gift of the Holy Spirit, who will teach us everything and offers his peace, unlike any other: "Not as the world gives do I give it to you. Do not let your hearts be troubled or afraid." It is a great comfort for us to know that when we are afraid, worried, or carry burdens and concerns, he offers us peace. Are we able to receive his peace and bring it to others? Or do we let anxiety and stress burden our hearts and minds? Let us open our hearts to receive his peace and, like Jesus, offer those who struggle his comfort and peace.

May 30 or June 2, 2019

ASCENSION OF THE LORD

A reading from the holy Gospel according to Luke   24:46–53

Jesus said to his disciples:
    "Thus it is written that the Christ would suffer
    and rise from the dead on the third day
    and that repentance, for the forgiveness of sins,
    would be preached in his name
    to all the nations, beginning from Jerusalem.
You are witnesses of these things.

And behold I am sending the promise of my Father upon you;
>   but stay in the city
>   until you are clothed with power from on high."

Then he led them out as far as Bethany,
>   raised his hands, and blessed them.
As he blessed them he parted from them
>   and was taken up to heaven.
They did him homage
>   and then returned to Jerusalem with great joy,
>   and they were continually in the temple praising God.

The Gospel of the Lord.

EXPLANATION OF THE READING

Jesus explains to his disciples how everything that was written about the Messiah—the Christ—in the Scriptures has been fulfilled in him. After he is taken up to his Father, the Holy Spirit—"the promise of my Father"— will come upon them, and they are to witness to all that they have seen. Until that time, they will continually praise God. We who have been baptized and confirmed have received the Holy Spirit, who calls us to witness to Christ. In the limitations of illness or old age, we may wonder how we can do this. Yet we have known the presence of Christ in good times and difficult times. We know that he has never abandoned us, and never will. We can witness to the power and faithfulness of God through Jesus Christ. And we can continually praise God.

June 2, 2019

SEVENTH SUNDAY OF EASTER

A reading from the holy Gospel according to John   17:20–26

Lifting up his eyes to heaven, Jesus prayed, saying:
  "Holy Father, I pray not only for them,
  but also for those who will believe in me through their word,
  so that they may all be one,
  as you, Father, are in me and I in you,
  that they also may be in us,
  that the world may believe that you sent me.
And I have given them the glory you gave me,
  so that they may be one, as we are one,
  I in them and you in me,
  that they may be brought to perfection as one,
  that the world may know that you sent me,
  and that you loved them even as you loved me.
Father, they are your gift to me.
I wish that where I am they also may be with me,
  that they may see my glory that you gave me,
  because you loved me before the foundation of the world.
Righteous Father, the world also does not know you,
  but I know you, and they know that you sent me.
I made known to them your name and I will make it known,
  that the love with which you loved me
  may be in them and I in them."

The Gospel of the Lord.

EXPLANATION OF THE READING

In today's Gospel Jesus prays for his disciples. We know that many of his followers end up abandoning, betraying, and forsaking him. How is he able to offer this prayer for them, knowing that they are not able to be faithful to him as a friend and faithful to the mission? The disciples do come back together as one, following the Resurrection. The feeling of abandonment and the act of abandoning others weigh heavily on the heart. When we are disappointed by the actions of others or by our own behavior, let us pray for the strength to forgive or to ask forgiveness and know the harmony and unity that come from our relationship with the Risen Christ.

June 9, 2019

PENTECOST

**A reading from the holy Gospel
according to John**   14:15–16, 23b–26

Jesus said to his disciples:
   "If you love me, you will keep my commandments.
And I will ask the Father,
   and he will give you another Advocate to be
      with you always.

"Whoever loves me will keep my word,
   and my Father will love him,
   and we will come to him and make our dwelling with him.
Those who do not love me do not keep my words;
   yet the word you hear is not mine
   but that of the Father who sent me.

"I have told you this while I am with you.
The Advocate, the Holy Spirit whom the Father will send in
    my name,
  will teach you everything
  and remind you of all that I told you."

The Gospel of the Lord.

Alternative reading: John 20:19–23

EXPLANATION OF THE READING

Jesus said, "Whoever loves me will keep my word, and my Father will love him, and we will come to him and make our dwelling with him." When we invite strangers, guests, and family to dwell in our homes, a lot of preparations need to be made, and the work of hospitality continues while company is in our home. When Jesus speaks about dwelling in us, he is referring to taking up residence. If a temporary guest changes our lives, how much more will having Jesus dwell with us permanently? For those who seek refuge in our homes and in our hearts, may we welcome them as we do the Father, Son, and Spirit.

Ordinary Time during Summer and Fall

June 16, 2019

Most Holy Trinity

A reading from the holy Gospel according to John   16:12–15

Jesus said to his disciples:
"I have much more to tell you, but you cannot bear it now.
But when he comes, the Spirit of truth,
he will guide you to all truth.
He will not speak on his own,
but he will speak what he hears,
and will declare to you the things that are coming.
He will glorify me,
because he will take from what is mine and declare it to you.
Everything that the Father has is mine;
for this reason I told you that he will take from what is mine
and declare it to you."

The Gospel of the Lord.

EXPLANATION OF THE READING

Jesus proclaims to his disciples that there is much more that he must tell them, but they could not bear hearing it now. What they hold now is enough. There will come a time for his followers to know this truth and it will be declared to them. The mission that Jesus began with his disciples is continued in us through the work of the Spirit. It is through the gifts of the Spirit that God's people, the Church, have been able to carry on the teachings and work of Jesus, and will continue do so. The Spirit also helps us each individually to contribute to the plan of God, whatever our condition of life may be. Though we may not always know or understand all that God has planned for us, there will be a time when it will be made known. May this be a time for us to deepen our trust in God's care for us.

June 23, 2019

Most Holy Body and Blood of Christ

A reading from the holy Gospel according to Luke 9:11b–17

Jesus spoke to the crowds about the kingdom of God,
   and he healed those who needed to be cured.
As the day was drawing to a close,
   the Twelve approached him and said,
   "Dismiss the crowd
   so that they can go to the surrounding villages and farms
   and find lodging and provisions;
   for we are in a deserted place here."
He said to them, "Give them some food yourselves."
They replied, "Five loaves and two fish are all we have,
   unless we ourselves go and buy food for all these people."
Now the men there numbered about five thousand.
Then he said to his disciples,
   "Have them sit down in groups of about fifty."
They did so and made them all sit down.
Then taking the five loaves and the two fish,
   and looking up to heaven,

he said the blessing over them, broke them,
and gave them to the disciples to set before the crowd.
They all ate and were satisfied.
And when the leftover fragments were picked up,
  they filled twelve wicker baskets.

The Gospel of the Lord.

EXPLANATION OF THE READING

In today's Gospel we hear about the feeding of more than five thousand
people. When all had eaten their fill, there were twelve baskets of food left
over. While this abundance in and of itself is significant, there is meaning
for us when we hear the number twelve in the Bible, particularly the twelve
tribes of Israel or the Twelve Apostles. The Twelve Apostles are given a role
in this miracle with the command "Give them some food yourselves." We,
too, are invited to collaborate with the Lord in his plan. The implication for
us is that no one is to be left wanting; in God's Kingdom, all will be fed.
May we always hunger for the abundant love of God.

June 30, 2019

THIRTEENTH SUNDAY
IN ORDINARY TIME

A reading from the holy Gospel according to Luke   9:51–62

When the days for Jesus' being taken up were fulfilled,
  he resolutely determined to journey to Jerusalem,
  and he sent messengers ahead of him.
On the way they entered a Samaritan village
  to prepare for his reception there, but they would not
    welcome him
  because the destination of his journey was Jerusalem.

When the disciples James and John saw this they asked,
  "Lord, do you want us to call down fire from heaven
  to consume them?"
Jesus turned and rebuked them, and they journeyed to
  another village.

As they were proceeding on their journey someone
  said to him,
  "I will follow you wherever you go."
Jesus answered him,
  "Foxes have dens and birds of the sky have nests,
  but the Son of Man has nowhere to rest his head."

And to another he said, "Follow me."
But he replied, "Lord, let me go first and bury my father."
But he answered him, "Let the dead bury their dead.
But you, go and proclaim the kingdom of God."
And another said, "I will follow you, Lord,
  but first let me say farewell to my family at home."
To him Jesus said, "No one who sets a hand to the plow
  and looks to what was left behind is fit for
  the kingdom of God."

The Gospel of the Lord.

EXPLANATION OF THE READING

In today's Gospel, we hear, "Foxes have dens and birds of the sky have nests, but the Son of Man has nowhere to rest his head." Is Jesus asking us to leave behind material goods, when those things can bring us familiarity and comfort? Not necessarily. He is inviting each of us to consider the value of the Kingdom of God versus the value of the comforts of this world. Discipleship is demanding and difficult. How do we manage being a disciple with the realities of our day-to-day life? From career and family responsibilities, to health problems and struggles, we seek to know how we are called to live our discipleship this day. Let us pray today to know what is truly valuable, and for all who seek a place to lay their head.

July 7, 2019

FOURTEENTH SUNDAY IN ORDINARY TIME

A reading from the holy Gospel according to Luke 10:1–9

At that time the Lord appointed seventy-two others
    whom he sent ahead of him in pairs
    to every town and place he intended to visit.
He said to them,
    "The harvest is abundant but the laborers are few;
    so ask the master of the harvest
    to send out laborers for his harvest.
Go on your way;
    behold, I am sending you like lambs among wolves.
Carry no money bag, no sack, no sandals;
    and greet no one along the way.
Into whatever house you enter, first say,
    'Peace to this household.'
If a peaceful person lives there,
    your peace will rest on him;
    but if not, it will return to you.
Stay in the same house and eat and drink what
        is offered to you,
    for the laborer deserves his payment.
Do not move about from one house to another.

Whatever town you enter and they welcome you,
    eat what is set before you,
    cure the sick in it and say to them,
    'The kingdom of God is at hand for you.'"

The Gospel of the Lord.

Long form: Luke 10:1–12, 17–20

EXPLANATION OF THE READING

There is something comforting in today's Gospel in that the disciples are sent out in pairs. No one individual bears the entirety of the responsibility, but we can rely on others to help us proclaim that the Kingdom of God is at hand. In living out our mission as a disciple, we are called to depend on one another for support, hospitality, and assistance. In a society that values self-reliance, this is countercultural. When we are baptized, we become part of the community that Christ formed to continue his work. When we come together as a community, may we be reminded that we are called to respond to our baptismal mission and find comfort in knowing we are not alone in this work.

July 14, 2019

FIFTEENTH SUNDAY IN ORDINARY TIME

A reading from the holy Gospel according to Luke   10:25–37

There was a scholar of the law who stood up to test
    Jesus and said,
    "Teacher, what must I do to inherit eternal life?"
Jesus said to him, "What is written in the law?
How do you read it?"

He said in reply,
   "You shall love the Lord, your God,
   with all your heart,
   with all your being,
   with all your strength,
   and with all your mind,
   and your neighbor as yourself."
He replied to him, "You have answered correctly;
   do this and you will live."

But because he wished to justify himself, he said to Jesus,
   "And who is my neighbor?"
Jesus replied,
   "A man fell victim to robbers
   as he went down from Jerusalem to Jericho.
They stripped and beat him and went off leaving
      him half-dead.
A priest happened to be going down that road,
   but when he saw him, he passed by on the opposite side.
Likewise a Levite came to the place,
   and when he saw him, he passed by on the opposite side.
But a Samaritan traveler who came upon him
   was moved with compassion at the sight.
He approached the victim,
   poured oil and wine over his wounds and bandaged them.
Then he lifted him up on his own animal,
   took him to an inn, and cared for him.
The next day he took out two silver coins
   and gave them to the innkeeper with the instruction,
   'Take care of him.

If you spend more than what I have given you,
   I shall repay you on my way back.'
Which of these three, in your opinion,
   was neighbor to the robbers' victim?"
He answered, "The one who treated him with mercy."
Jesus said to him, "Go and do likewise."

The Gospel of the Lord.

EXPLANATION OF THE READING

Who is my neighbor? We have come to know that our neighbor is anyone
who is hurting, not just in a physical manner but also emotionally,
socially, and spiritually. As a Church, we are called to bring Christ to the
peripheries, to find those who need healing. Every one of us has wounds
of one kind or another. There are times when we are the ones who are
among the marginalized and alone. It is our wounds that need to be
bound up; it is our body that needs care and rest. May we pray in
thanksgiving for those neighbors who allow us to feel less isolated,
who will not neglect us or pass us by this week.

July 21, 2019

SIXTEENTH SUNDAY IN ORDINARY TIME

A reading from the holy Gospel according to Luke   10:38–42

Jesus entered a village
   where a woman whose name was Martha welcomed him.
She had a sister named Mary
   who sat beside the Lord at his feet listening
      to him speak.

Martha, burdened with much serving, came to him and said,
  "Lord, do you not care
  that my sister has left me by myself to do the serving?
Tell her to help me."
The Lord said to her in reply,
  "Martha, Martha, you are anxious and worried about
    many things.
There is need of only one thing.
Mary has chosen the better part
  and it will not be taken from her."

The Gospel of the Lord.

EXPLANATION OF THE READING

We can certainly identify with Martha wanting to make sure the details
of hospitality are attended to and that our guests are well cared for
in our home. Martha, however, seems to be a little more than simply
worried about being a good host; she is frustrated that her sister is not
equally concerned. We can easily become annoyed with our family
and those closest to us. It can be difficult to accommodate the schedules
and plans of those in our household, and sometimes illness and weakness
can cause us to rely on people to do what we always did so carefully
ourselves. When we find ourselves anxious and frustrated with ourselves
or others, we can choose a better part. May we find peace and comfort
at the feet of our Lord, who enters our homes and hearts just as he did
in Bethany.

July 28, 2019

SEVENTEENTH SUNDAY IN ORDINARY TIME

A reading from the holy Gospel according to Luke 11:1–13

Jesus was praying in a certain place,
    and when he had finished,
  one of his disciples said to him,
  "Lord, teach us to pray just as John taught his disciples."
He said to them, "When you pray, say:
    Father, hallowed be your name,
      your kingdom come.
      Give us each day our daily bread
      and forgive us our sins
      for we ourselves forgive everyone in debt to us,
      and do not subject us to the final test."

And he said to them, "Suppose one of you has a friend
  to whom he goes at midnight and says,
  'Friend, lend me three loaves of bread,
  for a friend of mine has arrived at my house
    from a journey
  and I have nothing to offer him,'
  and he says in reply from within,
  'Do not bother me; the door has already been locked
  and my children and I are already in bed.
I cannot get up to give you anything.'

I tell you,
    if he does not get up to give the visitor the loaves
    because of their friendship,
    he will get up to give him whatever he needs
    because of his persistence.

"And I tell you, ask and you will receive;
    seek and you will find;
    knock and the door will be opened to you.
For everyone who asks, receives;
    and the one who seeks, finds;
    and to the one who knocks, the door will be opened.
What father among you would hand his son a snake
    when he asks for a fish?
Or hand him a scorpion when he asks for an egg?
If you then, who are wicked,
    know how to give good gifts to your children,
    how much more will the Father in heaven
    give the Holy Spirit to those who ask him?"

The Gospel of the Lord.

EXPLANATION OF THE READING

Some call this reading the parable of the insistent friend. It tells us about
how we are to approach God in prayer: with confidence and perseverance.
When we pray, we are often searching and asking God to take care of
our needs. Whenever we knock on that door, we must do so knowing
that God hears and will respond, and he will do it with gracious love,
not with annoyance. Even when we are offering the Lord prayers of
praise, thanksgiving, and even repentance, we should be as persistent
as we are with asking for what we need. God hears our prayers. We can
always trust that the door will open and the bread we need will be given.

August 4, 2019

EIGHTEENTH SUNDAY IN ORDINARY TIME

A reading from the holy Gospel according to Luke   12:13–21

Someone in the crowd said to Jesus,
   "Teacher, tell my brother to share the inheritance with me."
He replied to him,
   "Friend, who appointed me as your judge and arbitrator?"
Then he said to the crowd,
   "Take care to guard against all greed,
   for though one may be rich,
   one's life does not consist of possessions."

Then he told them a parable.
"There was a rich man whose land produced
     a bountiful harvest.
He asked himself, 'What shall I do,
   for I do not have space to store my harvest?'
And he said, 'This is what I shall do:
   I shall tear down my barns and build larger ones.
There I shall store all my grain and other goods
   and I shall say to myself, "Now as for you,
   you have so many good things stored up
     for many years,
   rest, eat, drink, be merry!"'
But God said to him,
   'You fool, this night your life will be demanded
     of you;
   and the things you have prepared,
     to whom will they belong?'

Thus will it be for all who store up treasure
   for themselves
   but are not rich in what matters to God."

The Gospel of the Lord.

EXPLANATION OF THE READING

The Gospel speaks of a rich man who is concerned about finding adequate space to store his harvest. This a completely reasonable thing to do; certain things are needed to sustain our life. The man is not being criticized for his wealth but rather for what he does with that it. He thinks it is all for him and his enjoyment. The warning of this story is that those who store up treasure for themselves alone are not rich in what matters to God. When God bestows a gift, it is for the benefit of the whole community. How have we benefitted from the gifts bestowed on others? What God-given gifts have we shared? In times of weakness, God blesses us with gifts for our well-being, but even those are also a gift to others. How can my blessings be a gift those around me?

August 11, 2019

NINETEENTH SUNDAY IN ORDINARY TIME

A reading from the holy Gospel according to Luke   12:35–40

Jesus said to his disciples:
   "Gird your loins and light your lamps
   and be like servants who await their master's
      return from a wedding,
   ready to open immediately when he comes and knocks.
Blessed are those servants
   whom the master finds vigilant on his arrival.
Amen, I say to you, he will gird himself,
   have them recline at table, and proceed to wait on them.

And should he come in the second or third watch
  and find them prepared in this way,
  blessed are those servants.
Be sure of this:
  if the master of the house had known the hour
  when the thief was coming,
  he would not have let his house be broken into.
You also must be prepared, for at an hour you
    do not expect,
  the Son of Man will come."

The Gospel of the Lord.

Long form: Luke 12:32–48

EXPLANATION OF THE READING

Be prepared! Like the servant who awaits his master's return from a wedding, we are called to be vigilant. What are we watching for? For our own master, Jesus Christ, who is with us now and will come again glory at the end of time. Like the servant, we do not know when the Lord's final arrival may come, but we do know that he is still among us. It takes energy and resilience to be able to stay awake and watch for him. May we always be ready to receive the Risen Christ when he comes to us. Let us be grateful for those in our community with watchful hearts, who are alert to the needs of others.

August 15, 2019

ASSUMPTION OF THE BLESSED VIRGIN MARY

A reading from the holy Gospel according to Luke   1:39–56

Mary set out
  and traveled to the hill country in haste

to a town of Judah,
   where she entered the house of Zechariah
   and greeted Elizabeth.
When Elizabeth heard Mary's greeting,
   the infant leaped in her womb,
   and Elizabeth, filled with the Holy Spirit,
   cried out in a loud voice and said,
   "Blessed are you among women,
   and blessed is the fruit of your womb.
And how does this happen to me,
   that the mother of my Lord should come to me?
For at the moment the sound of your greeting reached my ears,
   the infant in my womb leaped for joy.
Blessed are you who believed
   that what was spoken to you by the Lord
   would be fulfilled."

And Mary said:

   "My soul proclaims the greatness of the Lord;
      my spirit rejoices in God my Savior
      for he has looked with favor on his lowly servant.
   From this day all generations will call me blessed:
      the Almighty has done great things for me
      and holy is his Name.
      He has mercy on those who fear him
      in every generation.
   He has shown the strength of his arm,
      and has scattered the proud in their conceit.
   He has cast down the mighty from their thrones,
      and has lifted up the lowly.

He has filled the hungry with good things,
    and the rich he has sent away empty.
He has come to the help of his servant Israel
    for he has remembered his promise of mercy,
    the promise he made to our fathers,
    to Abraham and his children for ever."

Mary remained with her about three months
    and then returned to her home.

The Gospel of the Lord.

EXPLANATION OF THE READING

In today's Gospel, we hear Mary's canticle, a beautiful song of praise to God. The prayer begins with Mary's gratitude to God. She begins by praising God, "My soul magnifies the Lord," and then expressing joy, "And my spirit rejoices in God my Savior." How delightful for us to know that when we praise God, it is followed by joy! Is there anything that prevents you from finding the joy of God's presence in your daily life? In your own prayer, this week, how can you celebrate God as your Savior? How are you called to pray in a way that your soul magnifies the Lord?

August 18, 2019

TWENTIETH SUNDAY IN ORDINARY TIME

A reading from the holy Gospel according to Luke   12:49–53

Jesus said to his disciples:
    "I have come to set the earth on fire,
    and how I wish it were already blazing!
There is a baptism with which I must be baptized,
    and how great is my anguish until it is accomplished!
Do you think that I have come to establish peace on the earth?

No, I tell you, but rather division.
From now on a household of five will be divided,
   three against two and two against three;
   a father will be divided against his son
   and a son against his father,
   a mother against her daughter
   and a daughter against her mother,
   a mother-in-law against her daughter-in-law
   and a daughter-in-law against her mother-in-law."

The Gospel of the Lord.

EXPLANATION OF THE READING

Jesus comes to us as the Prince of Peace. How difficult, then, it is for us
to hear the words in today's Gospel regarding trials that will face the
disciples! Some decisions that we make as disciples will cause conflict,
even with our own families—"a father will be divided against his son . . .
a mother against her daughter . . . a mother-in-law against her
daughter-in-law." What happens when there is conflict in our family?
Are we able to disagree respectfully and offer compassion to those we
love? Let us pray for all those who live in division and conflict, that they
may find peace.

August 25, 2019

TWENTY-FIRST SUNDAY
IN ORDINARY TIME

A reading from the holy Gospel according to Luke   13:22–30

Jesus passed through towns and villages,
   teaching as he went and making his way to Jerusalem.
Someone asked him,
   "Lord, will only a few people be saved?"

He answered them,
   "Strive to enter through the narrow gate,
   for many, I tell you, will attempt to enter
   but will not be strong enough.
After the master of the house has arisen and locked the door,
   then will you stand outside knocking and saying,
   'Lord, open the door for us.'
He will say to you in reply,
   'I do not know where you are from.'
And you will say,
   'We ate and drank in your company and
      you taught in our streets.'
Then he will say to you,
   'I do not know where you are from.
Depart from me, all you evildoers!'
And there will be wailing and grinding of teeth
   when you see Abraham, Isaac, and Jacob
   and all the prophets in the kingdom of God
   and you yourselves cast out.
And people will come from the east and the west
   and from the north and the south
   and will recline at table in the kingdom of God.
For behold, some are last who will be first,
   and some are first who will be last."

The Gospel of the Lord.

EXPLANATION OF THE READING

"The last will be first and the first will be last." This often-quoted saying occurs only once in Scripture, in today's passage from Luke's account of the Gospel. Many of us have had the experience of waiting a long time to be called in a hospital emergency room when someone was rushed in ahead of us. Of course, we understand that the most serious illnesses or injuries require immediate attention, but when we are in pain or feeling sick, we still may feel that it's not quite fair. Whether our name is called first or we are the last in line, all are called to the Kingdom. Even when we seem to be an outcast, in last place, or even forgotten, we are invited to come and enter through the narrow door. May God's mercy, love, and patience guide our actions and our hearts this week.

September 1, 2019

TWENTY-SECOND SUNDAY IN ORDINARY TIME

A reading from the holy Gospel according to Luke   14:1, 7–14

On a sabbath Jesus went to dine
   at the home of one of the leading Pharisees,
   and the people there were observing him carefully.

He told a parable to those who had been invited,
   noticing how they were choosing the places
      of honor at the table.
"When you are invited by someone to a wedding banquet,
   do not recline at table in the place of honor.
A more distinguished guest than you may have
      been invited by him,
   and the host who invited both of you may approach
      you and say,
   'Give your place to this man,'
   and then you would proceed with embarrassment
   to take the lowest place.
Rather, when you are invited,
   go and take the lowest place
   so that when the host comes to you he may say,
   'My friend, move up to a higher position.'

Then you will enjoy the esteem of your companions
    at the table.
For everyone who exalts himself will be humbled,
    but the one who humbles himself will be exalted."
Then he said to the host who invited him,
    "When you hold a lunch or a dinner,
    do not invite your friends or your brothers
    or your relatives or your wealthy neighbors,
    in case they may invite you back and
        you have repayment.
Rather, when you hold a banquet,
    invite the poor, the crippled, the lame, the blind;
    blessed indeed will you be because of their inability to
        repay you.
For you will be repaid at the resurrection of the righteous."

The Gospel of the Lord.

EXPLANATION OF THE READING

At the time of Jesus, there were strict cultural rules regarding the order
of who is more important than others. While dining in the home of an
important man, Jesus offers a parable that challenges these rules and the
desire for public status they were built on. In doing so, he teaches those
gathered for the meal and us about life in the Kingdom of God. Those
who humble themselves in this world and offer hospitality to the poor
will be exalted and given the places of honor in the Kingdom. We are
called to be with those who are not honored by the world's rules: the
vulnerable, the fragile, and those who cannot pay us back with a reciprocal
invitation. Let us be grateful for those who offer us simple and
unassuming service this week. May the Lord allow us to serve with
that same humility.

September 8, 2019

TWENTY-THIRD SUNDAY IN ORDINARY TIME

A reading from the holy Gospel according to Luke   14:25–33

Great crowds were traveling with Jesus,
    and he turned and addressed them,
    "If anyone comes to me without hating his
        father and mother,
    wife and children, brothers and sisters,
    and even his own life,
    he cannot be my disciple.
Whoever does not carry his own cross and come after me
    cannot be my disciple.
Which of you wishing to construct a tower
    does not first sit down and calculate the cost
    to see if there is enough for its completion?
Otherwise, after laying the foundation
    and finding himself unable to finish the work
    the onlookers should laugh at him and say,
    'This one began to build but did not have
        the resources to finish.'
Or what king marching into battle would not first sit down
    and decide whether with ten thousand troops
    he can successfully oppose another king
    advancing upon him with twenty thousand troops?
But if not, while he is still far away,
    he will send a delegation to ask for peace terms.

In the same way,
anyone of you who does not renounce all his possessions
cannot be my disciple."

The Gospel of the Lord.

EXPLANATION OF THE READING

This week's Gospel focuses on the costs of being a disciple. What are those things that we hold on to, that seem to be important in our life? They could be material possessions, but sometimes we can cling to anger, contempt, or an attitude that does not allow us to be an authentic disciple. If we are to follow him, we will need to let go of those possessions, we need to surrender to our frustrations and annoyances so that we may more readily embrace the Kingdom. Have you ever let go of a possession that you did not need or an attitude that seemed too comfortable to do without? Doing that often gives us a feeling of freedom or lightness. Is there something that we would do well to let go of today?

September 15, 2019

TWENTY-FOURTH SUNDAY IN ORDINARY TIME

A reading from the holy Gospel according to Luke   15:1–10

Tax collectors and sinners were all drawing near
to listen to Jesus,
but the Pharisees and scribes began to complain, saying,
"This man welcomes sinners and eats with them."
So to them he addressed this parable.
"What man among you having a hundred sheep and losing
one of them
would not leave the ninety-nine in the desert
and go after the lost one until he finds it?

And when he does find it,
 he sets it on his shoulders with great joy
 and, upon his arrival home,
 he calls together his friends and neighbors and says to them,
 'Rejoice with me because I have found my lost sheep.'
I tell you, in just the same way
 there will be more joy in heaven over one sinner who repents
 than over ninety-nine righteous people
 who have no need of repentance.

"Or what woman having ten coins and losing one
 would not light a lamp and sweep the house,
 searching carefully until she finds it?
And when she does find it,
 she calls together her friends and neighbors
 and says to them,
 'Rejoice with me because I have found the coin that I lost.'
In just the same way, I tell you,
 there will be rejoicing among the angels of God
 over one sinner who repents."

The Gospel of the Lord.

Long form: Luke 15:1–32

EXPLANATION OF THE READING

Today's Gospel offers us three parables, each dealing with something lost being found: the found sheep, the found coin, and the forgiving father whose son returns to him. Why does Jesus offer us three parables? Would one not suffice? The first two parables illustrate that God will go to great lengths to find even one individual who is considered lost. The parable of the forgiving father shares with us the great compassion that God has for us when we sin and wander away from him. In each parable, there is an element of rejoicing when the lost has been found. In the third parable of the prodigal son, the celebration is interrupted by the older son who stands in judgment over his younger brother. When have you rejoiced when someone or something has been found? Have you ever let resentment get in the way of rejoicing with another?

September 22, 2019

TWENTY-FIFTH SUNDAY IN ORDINARY TIME

A reading from the holy Gospel according to Luke   16:10–13

Jesus said to his disciples:
  "The person who is trustworthy in very small matters
  is also trustworthy in great ones;
  and the person who is dishonest in very small matters
  is also dishonest in great ones.
If, therefore, you are not trustworthy with dishonest wealth,
  who will trust you with true wealth?
If you are not trustworthy with what belongs to another,
  who will give you what is yours?
No servant can serve two masters.
He will either hate one and love the other,
  or be devoted to one and despise the other.
You cannot serve both God and mammon."

The Gospel of the Lord.

Long form: Luke 16:1–13

EXPLANATION OF THE READING

Our culture would have us think that there is a fine line between honesty and dishonesty, but in today's Gospel, we hear about the role of the trustworthy servant. We are told that the dishonest person wastes the resources of the master. How do we use the resources God has given us?

When we make the most of those resources, we do the will of God. Jesus observes that human beings cannot serve two masters: if we are concerned about doing God's work, we cannot be loyal to the ways of the world. What choices have we made in the past? What choices face us now? May we be good and honest stewards of God's gifts this week.

September 29, 2019

TWENTY-SIXTH SUNDAY IN ORDINARY TIME

A reading from the holy Gospel according to Luke   16:19–31

Jesus said to the Pharisees:
    "There was a rich man who dressed in
        purple garments and fine linen
    and dined sumptuously each day.
And lying at his door was a poor man named Lazarus,
        covered with sores,
    who would gladly have eaten his fill of the scraps
    that fell from the rich man's table.
Dogs even used to come and lick his sores.
When the poor man died,
    he was carried away by angels to the bosom of Abraham.
The rich man also died and was buried,
    and from the netherworld, where he was in torment,
    he raised his eyes and saw Abraham far off
    and Lazarus at his side.
And he cried out, 'Father Abraham, have pity on me.
Send Lazarus to dip the tip of his finger in water
        and cool my tongue,
    for I am suffering torment in these flames.'

Abraham replied,

    'My child, remember that you received

    what was good during your lifetime

    while Lazarus likewise received what was bad;

    but now he is comforted here, whereas you

        are tormented.

Moreover, between us and you a great chasm is established

    to prevent anyone from crossing who might wish to go

    from our side to yours or from your side to ours.'

He said, 'Then I beg you, father,

    send him to my father's house, for I have five brothers,

    so that he may warn them,

    lest they too come to this place of torment.'

But Abraham replied, 'They have Moses and the prophets.

Let them listen to them.'

He said, 'Oh no, father Abraham,

    but if someone from the dead goes to them,

        they will repent.'

Then Abraham said, 'If they will not listen to

        Moses and the prophets,

    neither will they be persuaded if someone should

        rise from the dead.'"

The Gospel of the Lord.

EXPLANATION OF THE READING

The rich man is dressed in expensive garments and eats his fill, while Lazarus is covered in sores and he longs for any scrap of food that might fall to the ground. When these two men die, there is a reversal of fortunes. The rich man is tormented in the flames of the netherworld. He sees Lazarus, resting peacefully in the afterlife. While the rich man is not able to find relief for himself, he begs for his five brothers. He asks Abraham to send Lazarus to his brothers, to warn them to change their cold and heartless ways. Abraham reminds the rich man that both and his brothers have had the words of the Moses and the prophets to guide them. We, too, have had the prophets and even the Lord Jesus to teach us how God wants us to treat each other, particularly those in need. May our choices be made with compassion and allow us to share generously as we are called to do, and may we be grateful for those who extend compassion toward us.

October 6, 2019

TWENTY-SEVENTH SUNDAY IN ORDINARY TIME

A reading from the holy Gospel according to Luke 17:5–10

The apostles said to the Lord, "Increase our faith."
The Lord replied,
    "If you have faith the size of a mustard seed,
    you would say to this mulberry tree,
    'Be uprooted and planted in the sea,' and it would obey you.

"Who among you would say to your servant
    who has just come in from plowing or
        tending sheep in the field,
    'Come here immediately and take your place at table'?
Would he not rather say to him,
    'Prepare something for me to eat.
Put on your apron and wait on me while I eat and drink.
You may eat and drink when I am finished'?
Is he grateful to that servant because he did
        what was commanded?
So should it be with you.
When you have done all you have been commanded,
    say, 'We are unprofitable servants;
    we have done what we were obliged to do.'"

The Gospel of the Lord.

EXPLANATION OF THE READING

As Jesus instructs his disciples, they ask him to increase their faith. Have you ever felt, like the disciples, as though you needed more faith? How much faith is enough? How do you measure someone's faith? Is it fair to compare our faith to the faith of our neighbor? Jesus reminds the disciples that even with faith the size of a mustard seed, they would be able to do astonishing things. Even if they did not have faith as deep they would have liked, Jesus is letting them know that they can do great things with what God has given them. What have you been able to do in your life because of your faith? How does your faith sustain you now? Is there someone who has been a model of faith for you?

October 13, 2019

TWENTY-EIGHTH SUNDAY IN ORDINARY TIME

A reading from the holy Gospel according to Luke   17:11–19

As Jesus continued his journey to Jerusalem,
   he traveled through Samaria and Galilee.
As he was entering a village, ten lepers met him.
They stood at a distance from him and raised
     their voices, saying,
   "Jesus, Master! Have pity on us!"
And when he saw them, he said,
   "Go show yourselves to the priests."
As they were going they were cleansed.
And one of them, realizing he had been healed,
   returned, glorifying God in a loud voice;
     and he fell at the feet of Jesus and thanked him.
He was a Samaritan.
Jesus said in reply,
   "Ten were cleansed, were they not?

Where are the other nine?
Has none but this foreigner returned to give thanks to God?"
Then he said to him, "Stand up and go;
   your faith has saved you."

The Gospel of the Lord.

EXPLANATION OF THE READING

Has anyone ever offered you a heartfelt thank you? Even if we feel
embarrassed by accolades bestowed upon us or do not like being in the
limelight, we enjoy knowing that others appreciate our efforts. At the
same time, have you ever been taken for granted? Most of us can recall a
time when we thought we would hear words of thanks, but none was
spoken. In today's Gospel, we hear about ten lepers who were healed by
Jesus. Only one returns to express his gratitude for being cured. While
all were physically healed, the one that gave thanks is additionally blessed.
How does our own thanksgiving to God keep us in relationship with him?

October 20, 2019

TWENTY-NINTH SUNDAY
IN ORDINARY TIME

A reading from the holy Gospel according to Luke   18:1–8

Jesus told his disciples a parable
   about the necessity for them to pray always without
      becoming weary.
He said, "There was a judge in a certain town
   who neither feared God nor respected any human being.
And a widow in that town used to come to him and say,
   'Render a just decision for me against my adversary.'

For a long time the judge was unwilling,
    but eventually he thought,
    'While it is true that I neither fear God nor respect any
        human being,
    because this widow keeps bothering me
    I shall deliver a just decision for her
    lest she finally come and strike me.'"
The Lord said, "Pay attention to what
    the dishonest judge says.
Will not God then secure the rights of his chosen ones
    who call out to him day and night?
Will he be slow to answer them?
I tell you, he will see to it that justice is done
    for them speedily.
But when the Son of Man comes, will he find faith on earth?"

The Gospel of the Lord.

EXPLANATION OF THE READING

This parable seems to present prayer almost as nagging, as persistent as the woman demanding justice is. But our God is not like the judge in the parable. He does not answer prayers begrudgingly, relenting only because he is tired of our badgering. Furthermore, the judge in this parable is dishonest and cares for no one—clearly not like God. Still, Jesus uses the character of the judge to tell us that if someone like this dishonest judge can eventually honor the woman's request, how much more will our loving God hear our prayers and respond. Our God wants us to be like the widow in the parable, constantly seeking him and asking for what we need. There may be times when we might wonder if God hears our prayer. Do not lose heart, trust in him. Let us pray today, thy Kingdom come, thy will be done.

October 27, 2019

Thirtieth Sunday in Ordinary Time

A reading from the holy Gospel according to Luke   18:9–14

Jesus addressed this parable
    to those who were convinced of their own righteousness
    and despised everyone else.
"Two people went up to the temple area to pray;
    one was a Pharisee and the other was a tax collector.
The Pharisee took up his position and spoke
        this prayer to himself,
    'O God, I thank you that I am not like the rest
        of humanity—
    greedy, dishonest, adulterous—or even like
        this tax collector.
I fast twice a week, and I pay tithes on
        my whole income.'
But the tax collector stood off at a distance
    and would not even raise his eyes to heaven
    but beat his breast and prayed,
    'O God, be merciful to me a sinner.'
I tell you, the latter went home justified, not the former;
    for whoever exalts himself will be humbled,
    and the one who humbles himself will be exalted."

The Gospel of the Lord.

Explanation of the Reading

Have you ever compared yourself to someone else? Have you ever heard
someone brag about themselves and their life? In today's Gospel, we
hear about two men, a Pharisee and a tax collector. The Pharisee was a
man of status and importance in the community. The tax collector was

someone looked down on for collecting taxes from his own people—probably in an forceful way—on behalf of the Roman occupiers. The two men come before God. One asserts himself, taking a spot close to the front of the temple, while the other stays in the back with his head bowed. The Pharisee's prayer honors himself, while the tax collector's prayer humbly asks for God's mercy. There wasn't much room for God in the Pharisee's prayer, while the tax collector emptied himself before God. Let us look to the tax collector as a model of prayer this week, knowing that we need God in our lives.

November 1, 2019

ALL SAINTS

A reading from the holy Gospel according to Matthew   5:1–12a

When Jesus saw the crowds, he went up the mountain,
    and after he had sat down, his disciples came to him.
He began to teach them, saying:

> "Blessed are the poor in spirit,
>   for theirs is the Kingdom of heaven.
> Blessed are they who mourn,
>   for they will be comforted.
> Blessed are the meek,
>   for they will inherit the land.
> Blessed are they who hunger and thirst for righteousness,
>   for they will be satisfied.
> Blessed are the merciful,
>   for they will be shown mercy.
> Blessed are the clean of heart,
>   for they will see God.
> Blessed are the peacemakers,
>   for they will be called children of God.

Blessed are they who are persecuted for the sake
    of righteousness,
  for theirs is the Kingdom of heaven.
Blessed are you when they insult you and persecute you
and utter every kind of evil against you falsely
    because of me.
Rejoice and be glad,
  for your reward will be great in heaven."

The Gospel of the Lord.

EXPLANATION OF THE READING

There is great comfort found in the Beatitudes, Jesus' declaration of
who are considered blessed and joyful in God's Kingdom. The seventh
beatitude proclaims, "Blessed are the peacemakers: for they shall be
called the children of God." Peacemakers brings harmony and unity
where there is separation or discord. How are we called to be peacemakers? We are invited to live in peace with our families and friends.
We are called to keep peace between ourselves and God, to be children
of God, loving, obedient, and eager to do as God desires. When we
follow this path of peace, we are called children of God. Into what areas
of our lives can we bring the blessing of peace?

November 3, 2019

THIRTY-FIRST SUNDAY
IN ORDINARY TIME

A reading from the holy Gospel according to Luke   19:1–10

At that time, Jesus came to Jericho and intended
    to pass through the town.
Now a man there named Zacchaeus,
  who was a chief tax collector and also a wealthy man,
  was seeking to see who Jesus was;

but he could not see him because of the crowd,
    for he was short in stature.
So he ran ahead and climbed a sycamore tree
        in order to see Jesus,
    who was about to pass that way.
When he reached the place, Jesus looked up and said,
    "Zacchaeus, come down quickly,
    for today I must stay at your house."
And he came down quickly and received him with joy.
When they all saw this, they began to grumble, saying,
    "He has gone to stay at the house of a sinner."
But Zacchaeus stood there and said to the Lord,
    "Behold, half of my possessions, Lord,
        I shall give to the poor,
    and if I have extorted anything from anyone
    I shall repay it four times over."
And Jesus said to him,
    "Today salvation has come to this house
    because this man too is a descendant of Abraham.
For the Son of Man has come to seek
    and to save what was lost."

The Gospel of the Lord.

EXPLANATION OF THE READING

In the time of Jesus, the tax collector was not a popular figure. He worked for the Romans by collecting money from their fellow Jews. They could charge more than was required, which allowed them to make a large profit for themselves. The tax collector was considered a sinner. In the Gospel according to Luke, we hear about a chief tax collector named Zacchaeus. His wealth may have offered him a certain standing in the community, but physically he was quite short. He went to extreme lengths to see Jesus, even climbing a sycamore tree so he could see over the crowd. Jesus noticed him and called him to come down out of the tree. Jesus not only speaks to the man publicly, he offer him the honor of hosting Jesus as a houseguest. This honor causes discontent among the townspeople, but it prompts Zacchaeus to repent of his dishonest ways. Jesus rejoices in the sinner's salvation. How can we welcome Christ into our home this week?

November 10, 2019

THIRTY-SECOND SUNDAY IN ORDINARY TIME

A reading from the holy Gospel according to Luke 20:27, 34–38

Some Sadducees, those who deny that there is a resurrection,
   came forward.

Jesus said to them,
   "The children of this age marry and remarry;
   but those who are deemed worthy to attain to
      the coming age
   and to the resurrection of the dead
   neither marry nor are given in marriage.
They can no longer die,
   for they are like angels;
   and they are the children of God
   because they are the ones who will rise.
That the dead will rise
   even Moses made known in the passage about
      the bush,
   when he called out 'Lord,'

the God of Abraham, the God of Isaac,
    and the God of Jacob;
and he is not God of the dead, but of the living,
    for to him all are alive."

The Gospel of the Lord.

Long form: Luke 20:27–38

EXPLANATION OF THE READING

The Sadducees were a religious group within the Jewish community
at the time of Jesus. They interpreted the law of Moses strictly and
accepted no teachings not explicitly found there. This included belief in
the resurrection, which Jesus taught. When they ask Jesus to interpret
a particular teaching of Moses in light of a woman with seven husbands,
they are ridiculing belief in the afterlife. Jesus interpreted the same
scripture text, ignoring the story but proposing instead that as we
encounter our relationship with the living God, we encounter eternal
life. Let us look this week beyond what we encounter in the limits of our
earthly bodies, to envision the God of Life, who offers us his unlimited
grace, mercy, and life.

November 17, 2019

THIRTY-THIRD SUNDAY
IN ORDINARY TIME

A reading from the holy Gospel according to Luke   21:5–19

While some people were speaking about
    how the temple was adorned with costly stones and
        votive offerings,
    Jesus said, "All that you see here—
the days will come when there will not be left
a stone upon another stone that will not be thrown down."

Then they asked him,
    "Teacher, when will this happen?
And what sign will there be when all these things
        are about to happen?"
He answered,
"See that you not be deceived,
    for many will come in my name, saying,
    'I am he,' and 'The time has come.'
Do not follow them!
When you hear of wars and insurrections,
    do not be terrified; for such things must happen first,
    but it will not immediately be the end."
Then he said to them,
"Nation will rise against nation, and kingdom against
        kingdom.
There will be powerful earthquakes, famines, and plagues
    from place to place;
    and awesome sights and mighty signs will come from the sky.

"Before all this happens, however,
    they will seize and persecute you,
    they will hand you over to the synagogues and to prisons,
    and they will have you led before kings and governors
    because of my name.
It will lead to your giving testimony.
Remember, you are not to prepare your defense beforehand,
    for I myself shall give you a wisdom in speaking
    that all your adversaries will be powerless to resist or refute.
You will even be handed over by parents, brothers, relatives,
        and friends,
    and they will put some of you to death.

You will be hated by all because of my name,
   but not a hair on your head will be destroyed.
By your perseverance you will secure your lives."

The Gospel of the Lord.

EXPLANATION OF THE READING

How are we to think about the images that Luke's gospel offers us about the days to come? Jesus tells his followers of the challenges that await them not to cause alarm or fear, but to allow them to see beyond the persecution they will suffer to the security of life with our Lord. We, too, live in a time of challenges, and will rest secure in Christ. We have been assured all throughout Scripture that love is stronger that hate, light will overcome darkness, and life conquers death. May this knowledge offer you relief when you are feeling persecuted by pain or mislead by the misery of the world.

November 24, 2019

Our Lord Jesus Christ, King of the Universe

A reading from the holy Gospel according to Luke 23:35–43

The rulers sneered at Jesus and said,
   "He saved others, let him save himself
   if he is the chosen one, the Christ of God."
Even the soldiers jeered at him.
As they approached to offer him wine they called out,
   "If you are King of the Jews, save yourself."
Above him there was an inscription that read,
   "This is the King of the Jews."

Now one of the criminals hanging there reviled Jesus, saying,
    "Are you not the Christ?
Save yourself and us."
The other, however, rebuking him, said in reply,
    "Have you no fear of God,
    for you are subject to the same condemnation?
And indeed, we have been condemned justly,
    for the sentence we received corresponds to our crimes,
    but this man has done nothing criminal."
Then he said,
    "Jesus, remember me when you come into your kingdom."
He replied to him,
    "Amen, I say to you,
    today you will be with me in Paradise."

The Gospel of the Lord.

EXPLANATION OF THE READING

As they gather around the cross, those in the crowd and even one of the criminals beside him, taunt Jesus by calling him names. The title "King of the Jews" has been written to hang above his head, as if to mock him. In response, Jesus promises salvation to the other criminal who did recognize his kingship: "Jesus, remember me when you come into your kingdom." Those words do not belong to the good thief alone. Those are our words as well. We also want to dwell in the Kingdom. Every time we pray the Our Father, we say, "Thy Kingdom come." It offers us comfort and consolation, especially at those times when we are feeling vulnerable, alone, and afraid. Like the good thief, we too will hear that same promise, "I assure you: this day you will be with me in Paradise."

PATRON SAINTS

The saints and blesseds are our companions in prayer on our journey with Christ. Here we provide you with a list of health concerns and the saints chosen to intercede on a sick person's behalf before God the Father.

ILLNESS	SAINT(S)
A	
abdominal pains	Agapitus; Charles Borromeo; Emerentiana; Erasmus; Liborius
abortion, protection against	Catherine of Sweden
abuse victims	Adelaide; Agostina Pietrantoni; Fabiola; John Baptist de la Salle; Germaine Cousin; Godelieve; Jeanne de Lestonnac; Jeanne Marie de Maille; Joaquina Vedruna de Mas; Laura Vicuna; Maria Bagnesi; Monica; Rita of Cascia
AIDS patients	Aloysius Gonzaga; Thérèse of Lisieux; Peregrine Lazios
alcoholism	John of God; Martin of Tours; Matthias the Apostle; Monica; Urban of Langres
angina sufferers	Swithbert
appendicitis	Erasmus (Elmo)
apoplexy, apoplexies, stroke, stroke victims	Andrew Avellino; Wolfgang
arm pain; pain in the arms	Amalburga
B	
babies	The Holy Innocents; Maximus; Nicholas of Tolentino; Philip of Zell

bacterial disease and infection	Agrippina
barren women	Anthony of Padua; Felicity
barrenness, against	Agatha; Anne; Anthony of Padua; Casilda of Toledo; Felicity; Fiacre; Francis of Paola; Giles; Henry II; Margaret of Antioch; Philomena; Rita of Cascia; Theobald Roggeri
birth complications, against	Ulric
birth pains	Erasmus
blind people, blindness	Catald; Cosmas and Damian; Dunstan; Lawrence the Illuminator; Leodegarius; Lucy; Lutgardis; Odila; Parasceva; Raphael the Archangel; Thomas the Apostle
blood donors	Our Lady of the Thorns
bodily ills, illness, sickness	Alphais; Alphonsa of India; Angela Merici; Angela Truszkowska; Arthelais; Bathild; Bernadette of Lourdes; Camillus of Lellis; Catherine del Ricci; Catherine of Siena; Drogo; Edel Quinn; Elizabeth of the Trinity; Germaine Cousin; Hugh of Lincoln; Isabella of France; Jacinta Marto; John of God; Julia Billiart; Julia Falconieri; Juliana of Nicomedia; Louis IX; Louise de Marillac; Lydwina of Schiedam; Maria Bagnesi; Maria Gabriella; Maria Mazzarello; Marie Rose Durocher; Mary Ann de Paredes; Mary Magdalen of Pazzi; Michael the Archangel; Our Lady of Lourdes; Paula Frassinetti; Peregrine Laziosi; Philomena; Rafka Al-Rayes; Raphael; Teresa of Avila; Teresa Valse Pantellini; Terese of the Andes; Thérèse of Lisieux
breast cancer	Agatha; Aldegundis; Giles; Peregrine

breast disease, against	Agatha
breastfeeding women	Giles
broken bones	Drogo; Stanislaus Kostka

C

cancer patients; against cancer	Aldegundis; Giles; James Salomone; Peregrine Laziosi
child abuse victims	Alodia; Germaine Cousin; Lufthild; Nunilo
childbirth	Erasmus; Gerard Majella; Leonard of Noblac; Lutgardis; Margaret (or Marina) of Antioch; Raymond Nonnatus
childhood diseases	Aldegundis; Pharaildis
childhood intestinal diseases	Erasmus
children, convulsive	Guy of Anderlecht; John the Baptist; Scholastica
children, death of	Alphonsa Hawthorne; Angela of Foligno; Clotilde; Conception Cabrera de Annida; Cyriacus of Iconium; Elizabeth of Hungary; Elizabeth Ann Seton; Felicity; Frances of Rome; Hedwig; Isidore the Farmer; Joaquina Vedruna de Mas; Leopold the Good; Louis IX; Margaret of Scotland; Marguerite d'Youville; Matilda; Melania the Younger; Michelina; Nonna; Perpetua; Stephen of Hungary
children, sick	Beuno; Clement I; Hugh of Lincoln; Ubaldus Baldassini
children, stammering	Notkar Balbulus
colic	Agapitus; Charles Borromeo; Emerentiana; Erasmus; Liborius

contagious diseases	Robert Bellarmine; Sebastian
consumption	Pantaleon; Thérèse of Liseux
convulsions	John the Baptist; Willibrord
coughs, against	Blase; Quentin; Walburga
cramps, against	Cadoc of Llancarvan; Maurice; Pancras
cures from pain	Madron

D

deaf people, deafness	Cadoc of Llancarvan; Drogo; Francis de Sales; Meriadoc; Ouen
death	Michael the Archangel; Margaret (or Marina) of Antioch
death, happy	Joseph; Ulric
death, against sudden	Aldegundis; Andrew Avellino; Barbara; Christopher
disabled, handicapped	Alphais; Angela Merici; Gerald of Aurillac; Germaine Cousin; Giles; Henry II; Lutgardis; Margaret of Castello; Seraphina; Servatus; Servulus
drug abuse	Maximillian Kolbe
dying people, invoked by	Abel; Barbara; Benedict; Catherine of Alexandria; James the Lesser, Apostle; John of God; Joseph; Margaret (or Marina) of Antioch; Michael the Archangel; Nicholas of Tolentino; Sebastian
dysentary	Lucy of Syracuse; Polycarp

E

earache, against	Cornelius; Polycarp of Smyrna
epidemics	Godeberta; Lucy of Syracuse; Our Lady of Zapopan; Roch (Rocco)

epilepsy, epileptics	Alban of Mainz; Anthony the Abbot; Balthasar; Bibiana; Catald; Christopher; Cornelius; Dymphna; Genesius; Gerard of Lunel; Giles; Guy of Anderlecht; John Chrysostom; John the Baptist; Valentine; Vitus; Willibrord
ergotism, aginst	Anthony the Abbot
erysipelas	Anthony the Abbot; Benedict; Ida of Nivelles
expectant mothers	Gerard Majella; Raymond Nonnatus
eyes, eye diseases, eye problems, sore eyes	Aloysius Gonzaga; Augustine of Hippo; Clare of Assisi; Cyriacus of Iconium; Erhard of Regensburg; Herve; Leodegarius; Lucy of Syracuse; Raphael the Archangel; Symphorian of Autun

F

fainting, faintness	Urban of Langres; Ursus of Ravenna; Valentine
fever, against	Abraham; Adalard; Amalberga; Andrew Abellon; Antoninus of Florence; Benedict; Castorus; Claudius; Cornelius; Dominic of Sora; Domitian of Huy; Genevieve; Gerebernus; Gertrude of Nivelles; Hugh of Cluny; Liborius; Mary of Oignies; Peter the Apostle; Petronilla; Raymond Nonnatus; Severus of Avranches; Sigismund; Theobald Roggeri; Ulric; Winnoc
fistula	Fiacre
frenzy, against	Denis; Peter the Apostle; Ulric
foot problems; feet problems	Peter the Apostle; Servatus

G

gall stones	Benedict; Drogo; Florentius of Strasburg; Liborius
goiter	Blase
gout, against; gout sufferers	Andrew the Apostle; Coloman; Gregory the Great; Killian; Maurice

H

hangovers	Bibiana
head injuries	John Licci
headaches	Anastasius the Persian; Bibiana; Denis; Dionysius the Aeropagite; Gerard of Lunel; Gereon; Pancras; Stephen the Martyr; Teresa of Avila
health	Infant Jesus of Prague
healthy throats	Andrew the Apostle; Blase; Etheldreda; Godelieve; Ignatius of Antioch; Lucy of Syracuse; Swithbert
heart patients	John of God
hemorrhage	Lucy
hemorrhoid, piles	Fiacre
hernia	Alban of Mainz; Condrad Piacenzai; Cosmas and Damian; Drogo; Gummarus
herpes	George
hoarseness, against	Bernadine of Sienna; Maurus
hydrophobia (rabies)	Dominic de Silos; Guy of Anderlecht; Hubert of Liege; Otto of Bamberg; Sithney; Walburga

I

infertility, against	Agatha; Anne; Anthony of Padua; Casilda of Toledo; Felicity; Fiacre; Francis of Paola; Giles; Henry II; Margaret of Antioch; Philomena; Rita of Cascia
inflammatory disease	Benedict
intestinal diseases, against	Brice; Charles Borromeo; Emerentiana; Erasmus; Timonthy; Wolfgang
invalids, homebound	Roch (Rocco)

J

jaundice	Odilo

K

kidney disease, against	Benedict; Drogo; Margaret (or Marina) of Antioch; Ursus of Ravenna
kidney stones; gravel	Alban of Mainz
knee diseases or trouble	Roch (Rocco)

L

lame, the	Giles
leg diseases, leg trouble	Servatus
lepers, leprosy	George; Giles; Lazarus; Vincent de Paul
long life	Peter the Apostle
lumbago	Lawrence

M

mental illness	Benedict Joseph Labre; Bibiana; Christina the Astonishing; Drogo; Dymphna; Fillan; Giles; Job; Margaret

	of Cortona; Maria Fortunata Viti; Medard; Michelina; Osmund; Raphaela
migraine	Gereon; Severus of Avranches; Ulbadus Baldassini
milk, loss of by nursing women	Margaret of Antioch
miscarriage, against	Catherine of Sienna; Catherine of Sweden; Eulalia
miscarriage prevention	Catherine of Sweden
muteness	Drogo

N

near sightedness, short sightedness	Clarus, Abbot
nerve or neurological disease, against	Bartholomew the Apostle; Dymphna
nursing mothers	Concordia; Martina

O

obsession	Quirinus

P

pain relief	Madron
paralysis	Catald; Osmund; Wolfgang
physical spouse abuse, against; victims of spouse abuse, against	Rita of Cascia
plague, against	Adrian of Nicomedia; Catald; Cuthbert; Erhard of Regensburg; Francis of Paola; Francis Xavier; George; Genevieve; Gregory the Great; Macarius of Antioch; Roch (Rocco); Sebastian; Valentine; Walburga
poison sufferers	Benedict, Abbot; John the Apostle; Pirmin

pregnant women, pregnancy	Anne; Anthony of Padua; Elizabeth; Gerard Majella; Joseph; Margaret (or Marina) of Antioch; Raymond Nonnatus; Ulric

R

rape victims	Agatha; Agnes of Rome; Antona Messina; Dymphna; Joan of Arc; Maria Goretti; Pierina Morosini; Potamiaena; Solange; Zita
rheumatism, arthritis	Alphonus Maria de Liguori; Coloman; James the Greater; Killian; Servatus
respiratory problems	Bernadine of Sienna
ruptures, against Osmund	Drogo; Florentius of Strasburg;

S

scrofulous diseases	Balbina; Marculf; Mark the Evangelist
skin disease	Anthony the Abbot; George; Marculf; Peregrine Laziosi; Roch (Rocco)
skin rashes	Anthony the Abbot; George; Marculf; Peregrine Laziosi; Roch (Rocco)
sleepwalkers, sleepwalking	Dymphna
smallpox	Matthias
snakebite victims	Hilary; Paul
spasms	John the Baptist
sterility, against	Agatha; Anne; Anthony of Padua; Casilda of Toledo; Felicity; Fiacre; Francis of Paola; Giles; Henry II; Margaret of Antioch; Medard; Philomena; Rita of Cascia; Theobald Roggeri
stillborn children	Edmund

stomach disease, stomach trouble	Brice; Charles Borromeo; Erasmus; Timothy; Wolfgang
stroke	Andrew Avellino; Wolfgang
struma	Balbina; Marculf; Mark the Evangelist
surgery patients	Infant of Prague
syphilis	Fiacre; George; Symphoroian of Autun

T

throat diseases, against	Andrew the Apostle; Blaise; Etheldreda; Godelieve; Ignatius of Antioch; Lucy of Syracuse; Swithbert
toothaches	Apollonia; Christopher; Elizabeth of Hungary; Ida of Nivelles; Kea; Medard
tuberculosis	Pantaleon; Thérèse of Lisieux
twitching, against	Bartholomew the Apostle; Cornelius
typhus, against	Adelard

U

ulcers, against	Charles Borromeo; Job

V

venereal disease	Fiacre
verbal spousal abuse	Anne Marie Taigi; Godelieve; Monica
vertigo, against	Ulric

W

whooping cough, against	Blaise; Winoc
women in labor	Anne; Erasmus; John of Bridlington; Margaret (or Marina) of Antioch; Margaret of Fontana; Mary of Oignies
women who wish to be mothers	Andrew the Apostle
wounds	Aldegundis; Marciana; Rita of Cascia

Prayer Intentions

Use the space below to record the names of those you visit. Keep them in your personal prayers. Oftentimes, those you visit will ask you to pray for particular intentions. You can use this space to write down these intentions for continued prayer.

_____

_____

_____

_____

_____

_____

_____

_____

_____

_____

_____

_____

_____

_____

Prayer Intentions

Use the space below to record the names of those you visit. Keep them in your personal prayers. Oftentimes, those you visit will ask you to pray for particular intentions. You can use this space to write down these intentions for continued prayer.

_____

_____

_____

_____

_____

_____

_____

_____

_____

_____

_____

_____

_____

Prayer Intentions

Use the space below to record the names of those you visit. Keep them in your personal prayers. Oftentimes, those you visit will ask you to pray for particular intentions. You can use this space to write down these intentions for continued prayer.

_____

_____

_____

_____

_____

_____

_____

_____

_____

_____

_____

_____

Prayer Intentions

Use the space below to record the names of those you visit. Keep them in your personal prayers. Oftentimes, those you visit will ask you to pray for particular intentions. You can use this space to write down these intentions for continued prayer.

_____

_____

_____

_____

_____

_____

_____

_____

_____

_____

_____

_____

Prayer Intentions

Use the space below to record the names of those you visit. Keep them in your personal prayers. Oftentimes, those you visit will ask you to pray for particular intentions. You can use this space to write down these intentions for continued prayer.

_____

_____

_____

_____

_____

_____

_____

_____

_____

_____

_____

_____

_____

Prayer Intentions

Use the space below to record the names of those you visit. Keep them in your personal prayers. Oftentimes, those you visit will ask you to pray for particular intentions. You can use this space to write down these intentions for continued prayer.

_____

_____

_____

_____

_____

_____

_____

_____

_____

_____

_____

_____

_____

Prayer Intentions

Use the space below to record the names of those you visit. Keep them in your personal prayers. Oftentimes, those you visit will ask you to pray for particular intentions. You can use this space to write down these intentions for continued prayer.

_____

_____

_____

_____

_____

_____

_____

_____

_____

_____

_____

_____

_____

_____